PRO
Through
PEOPLE

PROFITS *Through* PEOPLE

How to develop your staff
to give you more

RON JOHNSON

Hutchinson
Business
Books

First published in Great Britain by
Business Books Limited
An imprint of Century Hutchinson Limited
20 Vauxhall Bridge Road, London, SW1V 2SA

Century Hutchinson Australia (Pty) Limited
20 Alfred Street, Milsons Point, Sydney,
New South Wales 2061, Australia

Century Hutchinson New Zealand Limited
PO Box 40-086, 32-34 View Road, Glenfield,
Auckland 10, New Zealand

Century Hutchinson South Africa (Pty) Limited
PO Box 337, Bergvlei 2012, South Africa

British Library Cataloguing in Publication Data
Johnson, Ron *1937–*
Profits through people.
1. Organisations. personnel. In-service training
I. Title
658.3′124

ISBN 0-09-174383-4

Typeset in Sabon by Tek Art Ltd, Croydon, Surrey

Printed and bound in Great Britain by
The Guernsey Press Co. Ltd., Guernsey, Channel Islands

Contents

Preface

The major factor that separates your firm from the other firms in the field is the people who work for it, especially the senior people, including you. This book is about how to develop your firm, or your department, by developing the skills of your people – and of yourself, too.

Developing ideas for the market-place, raising the capital you require, acquiring the premises, plant and machinery, making and selling your output, managing the money and all the relationships involved in a successful business – in the end, all this depends on the company's top man or woman and the people brought together to run the business as co-directors, partners and employees.

My earlier book, *How to Manage People* (Ron Johnson, Business Books, 1984) explains in simple terms how to recruit, train and manage people in a small to medium-sized firm. *Profits Through People* explains in greater detail how to develop the competence of yourself and your people to the full, so that they feel capable and confident in their work and keen to help the firm prosper. There is plenty of evidence that, apart from overwhelming external factors, this is the key to long-term success.

Helping people learn is much more than simply sending them off on courses. Off-the-job education and training has its place, but there is much that can be learned only on the job and from your firm's *own staff*. It is very important to recognize the need for this learning, and to encourage everyone to get involved in improving the competence and effectiveness of the firm. You will need to set an example, and motivate your people to follow.

Over a period of time, the improvement could prove dramatic. But don't expect instant results.

If you are the chief executive, you should find all of the book useful, but it is wise to focus on one particular area of the firm's activity to begin with – the one where you consider that real improvements are required.

If you are a director or senior manager in charge of a particular function within the firm, this will influence your choice of the most useful sections for you.

Having selected an area of the firm's activity where you would like to see improvements, look this up in the index and work through the relevant parts of the book. This should allow you to see which of your people can help overcome the problems that concern you, and what they need to learn to tackle them. Then turn to the index again to find sections of the book that deal with the kind of learning that is required (eg, acquiring manual skills or negotiating skills).

There is really no great mystery about how people learn, and a simple explanation of the main points is given in Chapter 13. The main problem is that we do not always think clearly enough about what we need to know and be able to do in order to succeed, so the first part of this book is devoted to helping you think through the various aspects of your business, so that you can see just where some effort and expenditure on learning will pay off. Once you see this, ways of learning and helping people learn should be obvious.

The second part of the book is concerned with some of the specific areas you will probably wish to tackle, and provides guidance on how to achieve this learning *cost-effectively* and *with the minimum of hassle. Profits Through People* has been written for managers, not trainers, and does not give detailed instructions on how to set up and run training courses.

Remember that training is not an end in itself, but a means of improving people's ability to perform, and to contribute to the profitability and survival of the enterprise. When your people have the skills, they need to be motivated as well: learning how to achieve this is paramount.

I am grateful to Robin Williams, John Bayley, Geoff Smith and John Annett for many helpful comments and discussions during the writing of this book.

RON JOHNSON

CHAPTER 1

People – the Source of Excellence

WHERE DOES SUCCESS COME FROM?

What does the success of your enterprise depend on? Before you read much further, jot down a few of your own ideas on this. Whether you are the managing director or a sectional manager, it is worth spending some time taking an overview of your company, its strengths and its weaknesses, its opportunities and the threats it faces.

Do you have a unique and wonderful product or service so that customers beat a path to your front door? Do you have an inexpensive source of raw materials, an advantageous loan or a very efficient system, so that your products or services are very competitively priced? Do you have an efficient production system that can manufacture quality products in a cost-effective manner? Or a broad customer base and good contacts with your customers to keep abreast of their requirements?

If you have these excellent arrangements, how did you get them? When you think about it, you will realize that these came about through your own efforts (perhaps with advice), and through the efforts of the people who work with you. Furthermore, if you want these successful arrangements to continue and to develop in line with the changing scene, this can happen only through the efforts you and your people make. The best systems will come to naught if the people 'running' them are not capable of doing so or are not motivated to do a good job.

If your firm or section is lacking in one or more of these key areas, that must indicate a priority for action on your part. Do you know which of your people make the key decisions in each area? Are you sure that they are competent to do the job expected of them, and that they really want to succeed in it?

QUALITY PRODUCTS AND SERVICES

The list of areas to be considered may be different for your firm, but no doubt some of the above ideas will apply, and you will be able to add some of your own. Now let's look at particular areas in turn.

First of all, consider the quality of your products and services. How did this come about? Did you or one of your people have an idea for a product or service, or did you notice a 'gap' in the market and think up a way of filling it? Once the type of product was decided, how did you set about designing it, and producing it at the required quality and price? How do you maintain this quality and competitive edge?

It's easy to see that the abilities of yourself, and probably of one or two of your key people, are crucial in this process. If the products and/or services you design do not match the needs of the customer, you're sunk. What is more, we live in a world that is changing, and in most cases your products and services must change as well. Together with your key people, you must have the ability to adapt to change: to modify your products and services if necessary, reduce price, increase quality, and so forth.

In matching your output to the needs of the market-place, you and your people must keep on learning and developing. If you want to stop learning and developing, think seriously about retirement. Find something else to do, but don't try to run a business – it's not fair on your customers and employees. Nothing is more important in your business than staying in tune with your customers.

What steps do you take to keep in step with your customers? Who asks them precisely what they require and how their requirements might change (eg, as their own business changes)? Unless they are properly briefed – and de-briefed – your salespeople will not be providing this information in a reliable way.

COMPETITIVE PRICING

How do you achieve a competitive price, and how do you keep it competitive? The price you can charge for your products or service depends on what the market will bear, but the lower limit is set by the costs you incur. There may be little room for manoeuvre on the price you pay for your raw materials, but if there is, then the skills of the individual in your organization who negotiates the price, quality and delivery dates of these materials will be crucial to your product price control. (By the way, it is no good talking about price without talking about quality: no skill is required to get poor quality raw materials cheaply.)

In business, virtually every cost you incur – buildings, machinery, fuel, paper and books, interest charges, raw materials and, above all, your employees – must be paid for out of income from sales. Hence every item, down to the last paper clip, adds to the cost of your products and services. In practice, when you go through a list of cost items, some will assume much greater importance than others. But in every case, you or one of your people will have some influence on the costs incurred. Who ensures that you have the best value loans, optimum leases on buildings, and optimum terms on machinery purchase or hire?

Who ensures that you have the right stocks of raw materials or finished goods (enough materials to keep the plant running and finished goods to meet demand, but not enough to incur unnecessary interest charges or capital tied up)? Failure to attend to these matters loses the firm money or jacks up the price of the output (which may cost the firm more money through lost sales). People need to be competent at dealing with these issues.

Examine the way products are made or services provided in your organization, and you will probably see that the scope for cost escalation is enormous. Machine down time, inadequate quality, unproductive use of employee time – you name it, and you'll probably find it. Don't be tempted to overcome problems like this by introducing elaborate management control systems. They may seem to work in the short run, but they could easily sap the enthusiasm of your workforce – and that is too high a price to pay.

If you want to improve the productivity of your people, there are three simple steps you must take. First, take yourself in hand. Make sure you are willing to learn, listen and improve your own performance. Second, take your people along with you. Inspire them with the enthusiasm you have to make the firm a success, and let them contribute to it with their ideas as well as their labour. Third, help them get the training and development they need to become fully competent at their jobs, and able to build on their abilities.

GENERATING INCOME

Generating income is about getting the goods and services to the customer, clinching a sale and collecting the cash. If you are selling goods for the public through retailers, you have a double objective. First of all, the goods must be attractive to the ultimate customer, but in the meantime, there must be a good deal for the retailer – and for you.

Whether you deliver your own products or not, you need people responsible for seeing that goods get to their destination in good time and in good condition, or that services are provided on time and in a satisfactory manner. Once again the competence of the people with such responsibilities is crucial to the success of your enterprise. Don't forget that the people who answer the telephone or reply to written enquiries are in the front line of your dealings with customers, not just the people labelled 'Sales'. In other words, there are an awful lot of people concerned with income generation – or lack of it – in your firm.

Although in some businesses sales are achieved on a casual basis, often the 'bread and butter' income is from repeat orders, or orders from people who have been recommended by other customers. To get, and keep, business like that is a matter of that peculiar quality called 'goodwill'. Goodwill is a lot more than producing goods of the right quality at the right price, place and time, with good follow-up service or prompt replies to queries. It is all of these things plus the feeling that this is the kind of firm to do business with, because the people are helpful; they go the extra mile; they do their best to help out even though there may be no immediate pay-off; they know what they are talking about, and can be trusted. Is your firm like that?

GETTING KNOWN

It only pays to advertise if your method is appropriate. Does your method reach potential customers? Does it project the right image? Is the cost commensurate with the value? How did you decide on the medium, the message, the format of your advertisement and the level of expenditure? This is not an area where you can afford mistakes or inefficiency. Even if you use the help of outside specialists, some of these key decisions must be made in-house. How did your firm secure the in-house competence to do this job to full effect?

This book is not a monograph on advertising, marketing or merchandising, but there is no doubt that unless your firm takes steps to be competent in these areas, it will run into trouble before long.

MANAGING MONEY

There are two major financial problems that lead to the failure of a firm: failure to match expanding production with expanding sales, and lack of control over cash flow so that insufficient funds are available to meet bills, even though the products and services may be profitable. Smaller firms in particular tend to identify their initial potential customers quite well, but as their production increases they find that they need to find new customers for their products, or to extend the range of their products or services to their existing customers. Failure to do this means that the firm cannot sell what it produces, and disaster follows.

It is therefore essential to have someone in your organization with his or her finger on the pulse of the financial situation, who knows how to monitor income and expenditure, and, above all, who can forecast the likely cash flow many months ahead. This individual must work closely with whoever deals with marketing and sales matters in your organization. Income from projected sales will not come if you are getting close to saturating your existing customers' demands, or if your product no longer satisfies your customers in some important respect.

In the final analysis, it is you, the boss, who must have a firm grip on the financial situation, and make decisions based on your assessments of the information you have. Thus, you must ensure that you are presented with the financial data you need to keep abreast of the state of the business. The frequency with which you have to review the financial position and the details you require depend on the nature of the goods or services you provide, and the kinds of decision you have to make. But whatever the business, it is essential that your money matters are handled efficiently and accurately. Ensuring that you have a competent person undertaking this work is crucial to your firm's *survival*, let alone its profitability.

This has been a superficial review of some of the key factors which make or break firms, but in every case there are some people in your firm (not forgetting you) who make decisions and take actions crucial to success. In a small firm, several of the roles described above may be done by the same person, but this does not make it any less important that the jobs should be done properly. There are two questions you must face up to:

- Do your people want the firm to succeed?
- Do your people have the competence to make the firm succeed?

Apart from some external calamity or windfall, it is not the investment, location or the equipment in your firm that makes the difference between success or failure; it is the enthusiasm and competence of you and of your people. Given this enthusiasm and competence, you and your team will be able to match your products and services to the market, satisfy the customers, raise the necessary capital, choose the optimum location and equipment, and so on. Without that enthusiasm and competence, all the investment and fine equipment will count for nothing.

Excellence in business comes only through people. Paying attention to the people in your organization is not an act of charity, it is sound business sense. It is the only way to secure lasting success.

ACTION GUIDELINES

1. Write down the parts of your operation which you consider crucial to success.
2. Say what you consider success depends on in each of these areas.
3. Make a list of the people responsible for taking the decisions and carrying out the tasks that are essential to success. Alongside each name, jot down the level of competence you think is needed for the person to be effective.
4. Make a note of how you might help each of the people you have identified to achieve the ability that he or she needs to be fully effective.
5. Decide how you might make a start in motivating your people to give their best.

CHAPTER 2

MARKETING AND SELLING

WHO IS INVOLVED?

The importance of marketing and selling has been stressed in Chapter 1. This chapter is concerned with how you can train the people in your firm who identify your customers, define their requirements, convert this information into viable products and services, present your firm and its services and products to the customers, make sales and follow up with after-sales services.

If you are serious about developing people to make your business successful, run down the checklist in Figure 1 (on page 8) carefully and answer each question. If you know your business, this should not take long for a small to medium-sized firm. If it does take you a long time, this is probably a priority area for attention.

As set out, this questionnaire asks you to specify – by name or job title – the people concerned with getting things done or presenting the image of your firm and its wares. The next step is to consider whether they are properly motivated and equipped to undertake this task. (The question of motivation is dealt with in Chapter 14.) If you find that some important question concerned with marketing and sales in your company does not appear in the checklist, add this at the end, and answer it along with the others.

LEARNING NEEDS

Having identified the individual(s) concerned, write down what you think they need to know and be able to do to be successful. You may need to talk to some of the people concerned about how they see their job and what is required. You could learn a lot by doing this, and it might help you when you come to develop the business in this area in the future. Don't forget, as we shall see later, that such conversations also help motivate your people to do their best for the firm.

Figure 1 Marketing and sales checklist

Who identifies the customers for each of your products/ services?

Who ensures that each product or service is properly geared to the market in terms of quality, size, price, etc?

Who ensures that realistic sales targets are set and reached?

Who is responsible for selling? Are these people all properly trained?

Who ensures that your advertising and other promotional activities are geared to the markets and products/services on offer?

Who ensures that the sales effort is properly supported by the delivery of goods and/or services – including after-sales service where appropriate?

Which of your staff can affect the 'image' of your firm? Are they all projecting the right image, or do some need training?

Which of your staff, not directly involved in selling, can crucially affect the performance of the marketing and sales effort? Do they all give the necessary support?

We shall consider in more detail later how people can be helped to acquire the skills and knowledge they require, but you may well find that simply by talking these things through you can find ways of helping people, there and then, to do the job more effectively. You may also recognize that there is someone else around who can help that individual to improve performance. Put them together for a while to work on this.

Don't think of training as simply sending people off on courses. Training is about helping people on the job to improve performancc by giving them information, talking through with them how the job can be done and demonstrating to them the best way of doing things. Don't forget to listen to their ideas as well.

FINDING THE CUSTOMER

Let us consider the questions in the checklist and see how these ideas might work out in practice. Who identifies the customers? What skills do they need? Presumably you get feedback from the people who are buying your products or using your services – are they satisfied, or would they like something a bit different? Are they turning to a competitor who produces larger/smaller/better/cheaper products than yours? What kind of people buy your wares (eg, teenagers or middle-aged mums, pensioners or young men)? If your customers are organizations, are they large or small, public bodies or private firms? What business are they in?

Are there similar people/organizations to whom you could be selling? What other form of market intelligence do you have? At some stage, you may well find it important to build up 'profiles' on important clients (ie, simple descriptions of their key features).

Do remember that 'organizations' as such do not make buying decisions: these decisions are taken by individuals, and a key part of the strategy is to identify who makes the purchasing decisions, and who has a say in them. The people in your firm responsible for promotion and sales must be able to identify the key individuals in your client organization, to assess their needs and priorities, and to pitch your promotion and sales activities accordingly.

The person we are talking about should know what sort of information you need about your customers, how to gather it, interpret it and use it to ensure that you exploit new market-places as your capacity to produce expands, or as some of your existing markets decline for one reason or another. This individual can learn a lot from books (eg, *How to Win Profitable Business*, Tom Cannon, Business Books, 1984), and by talking through the issues with other senior people in the business. If this is likely to be a major concern in your case, it might be worth arranging for the individual to attend a training course, provided he or she considers it worthwhile.

OPTIMUM PRODUCTS AND SERVICES

The next question – about gearing the products and services to the needs of the market – is often the hardest part. Sometimes we are reluctant to change the products and services we have already – so carefully – designed and provided. It may also be difficult to persuade people who do not come into direct contact with the customers that any change is needed. In order to counter this last problem, it makes sense to involve your production people in discussions about new or modified products, not only so that they can comment on the feasibility and costs of proposed changes, and on the time it will take to bring about the change, but also to gain their wholehearted commitment to the change-over.

It is amazing how often things go smoothly when people think it makes sense, but when they have real doubts about them, even the simplest change-overs seem fraught with problems. We tend to shrug off such problems as 'teething troubles', but in most cases they are caused by a lack of planning or of commitment, or both. The planning involves ensuring that everyone has the knowledge and skills needed to operate the new procedures and any new machinery involved.

Thus, people who have responsibility for matching the firm's products and services to the market-place not only need to use the market intelligence referred to in the previous chapter, but also need the ability to liaise effectively with the people within your firm responsible for implementing changes. Once prototype products are available, these individuals will probably be involved in test marketing and assessing customer reaction. Do they have the skills to conduct such a study and to interpret the results reliably?

SALES TARGETS

There is no magic formula for setting realistic targets. It is a matter of considering each of your potential customers and trying to estimate how much they will buy over a given period, if your products and services are competently presented and sold. There are two pieces of information which can help you. First, what have they bought before, and how did they like and use these? Second, are they likely to buy the same again, or has something happened which will alter their requirements from you (eg, a competitor may have entered the field or a key client company changed the way it works so that its requirements for your products or services have changed)?

The time interval over which you collate and review sales figures will vary from firm to firm. In some firms you will want daily figures, in other cases weekly or even monthly (eg, if you are in the business of making and selling a few high-value items each week). Reviewing sales figures too often wastes everybody's time and leads to frustration, but the frequency must allow you to monitor progress in time to take remedial action at the right moment when the need arises.

Since your cash flow forecasts depend on realistic assessments of future sales, the people in your firm responsible for this need to be reasonably accurate in forecasting sales potential and setting these figures as targets. Apart from any formal training in marketing, you may well find that if you and two or three of your people sit down from time to time to discuss your customers and competitors, you can improve your understanding of the market and, hence, your sales forecasts.

If you want to motivate your salespeople, see that their targets are achievable with effort. Targets set too low allow people to slacken off and lose their edge. Targets set too high cause frustration, anger and opting out. If the salespeople you have can achieve targets based on what your customers are likely to buy, all is well. If they fail to do this, is it either because you do not have enough salespeople, or because they are not good at selling or organizing their time, or because the products/services are not up to scratch or relevant, or because the back-up they receive is inadequate?

Another key to motivating your salespeople is to ensure that as far as possible they set their own targets in discussion with their immediate manager, and in the light of the information you have about the market-place and what they can realistically be expected to achieve. Wherever possible, see that there is a set of written-down sales objectives with target dates agreed between the salesperson and his or her boss, and that performance against these objectives is discussed regularly at sensible intervals.

When you have sold all you can to your existing customers, you need to look for new ones. This may be done either by getting someone to concentrate on this, or by making it part of the responsibility of each of your salespeople. Recognize that the person concerned may need some training and coaching to develop this ability to break new ground; to contact a new customer and make a sale.

If product displays and merchandising are important in your business, then the skills of the people responsible are also crucial. Remember that if your people need to be better at merchandising, selling or organizing their time, this is something you can tackle through training and coaching. Quality of output is dealt with in Chapter 5, and back-up services in Chapter 6.

SALESPEOPLE

The kind of salespeople you have depends on the nature of your business. If you are a retailer, for example, then you will be particularly concerned with the sales assistants, and should draw up a simple list of the tasks involved in the job, and then ensure that every person you employ in that role is trained to undertake each of the tasks competently. (Some examples of simple checklists are included in Figures 2 to 6, but you should make up your own.) Methods of training will be covered in later chapters.

As mentioned above, in most situations salespeople are motivated, in part, by sales targets, and their skills in selling can be considerably enhanced by on-the-job coaching (see Chapter 15). Remember that people learn best when you emphasize their successes, rather than concentrate on their failures. Where you do need to correct a salesperson on the job, remember three things:

- Have the talk in private
- Emphasize the error of the *deed*, don't denigrate the person
- End by encouraging the individual to do better next time, and expressing confidence in his or her ability to do so.

Figure 2 Sales assistant checklist (non-food)

The sales assistant must be able to:

Create the right environment
Help the customer feel at ease
Help customers select goods
Answer customer queries
Close the sale
Maintain security discreetly
Wrap goods or place in bags
Clean and lay out goods for sale
Maintain attractive display area
Check stock position
Price goods correctly
Operate the till
Handle money quickly and accurately
Give change correctly
Deal with cheques and credit cards
Deal with refunds and complaints

Figure 3 Sales assistant checklist (food)

The sales assistant must be able to:

Help customers select goods
Answer customer queries
Maintain security discreetly
Cut and slice food
Wrap food
Clean and lay out goods for sale
Maintain attractive display area
Check store position
Price goods correctly
Rotate stock
Observe sell-by dates
Operate the till
Handle money quickly and accurately
Give change correctly
Deal with cheques and credit cards
Deal with refunds and complaints

Figure 4 Industrial salesperson checklist

The industrial salesperson must be able to:

Organize his or her customer records for
– prospecting
– progress chasing
– gathering market intelligence
Keep customer records up to date
Speak about/demonstrate all the products for sale
Make appointments and organize sales visits
Close sales
Give reasonable quotes on prices and delivery dates
Negotiate discounts at appropriate rates
Make new contacts and obtain new customers
Plan ahead a schedule of visits
Forecast likely sales with reasonable accuracy
Meet sales targets
Maintain a balance in sales of different products

In addition, to stay on top the industrial salesperson needs to know about, and be constantly updated on:

All the firm's products and services
How each of the firm's products and services can be used
Competitors' products and services
Each customer's business, and where it is likely to go
The market within which each customer operates, and how this is likely to change
Selling and planning methods

Figure 5 Retail manager's checklist

The retail manager must be able to:

Assess the quality and value of merchandise
Maintain satisfactory stock levels
Ensure proper storage of goods and stock rotation
Ensure proper care of perishable, fragile, dangerous and edible goods
Ensure goods reach point of sale in acceptable condition
Supervise preparation and/or processing procedures
Control overheads and expenditure
Calculate ratios and other statistics as necessary
Ensure adherence to security procedures in relation to staff, customers, store, goods and cash
Carry out appropriate procedures in case of suspected theft
Ensure proper till and cashing-up procedures are observed
Ensure adherence to all hygiene, health and safety procedures, and 'good housekeeping'
Sell positively and competently
Maintain friendly, helpful attitude to customers
Use product knowledge to build confidence and increase sales
Introduce promotional lines and display effectively
Cope effectively with complaints
Supervise presentation of goods, pricing and ticketing
Review and maintain effective shop layout
Conduct induction training for all new staff
Train staff in customer relations and selling, hygiene and safety practices, product knowledge and use, and security procedures
Plan and allocate staff to maximize effect

In addition, the retail manager must maintain a working knowledge of:

All statutory requirements regarding retailing
Trade developments and changes
Middle-management skills

Figure 6 Telephone salesperson's checklist

The telephone salesperson must be able to:

Adhere to a sales programme
Maintain customer records and prepare for each call
Trace the 'purchase decision-makers' in the customer organization
Speak clearly and concisely on the telephone
Open up a constructive conversation on the telephone
Maintain a cool and constructive attitude to customers
Make contact with the purchase decision-makers
Present the services/products clearly, quickly and attractively
Obtain all relevant details from the customer
Ensure that action is jointly agreed wherever possible
Close a conversation in a positive, encouraging manner
Maintain proper records of telephone contacts with clients
Ensure follow-up action taken after each call

And where appropriate:

Receive telephone enquiries and convert these into sales opportunities
Operate computer terminals (eg, to obtain client information about products and services, or to make bookings on real-time system)

PROMOTIONAL ACTIVITIES

Your products and services can be promoted in a variety of ways. The problem is deciding which methods will reach your potential customer persuasively and cost-effectively. Who makes such decisions in your firm? How much does this person know about the advertising media you can use; how much it will cost; the relative merits of advertisements in different periodicals or newspapers; the value of leaflets inserted in journals; the impact of different kinds of packaging, window displays, etc?

If these are matters in which you are expert, you must ensure that your knowledge and experience are passed on (by coaching – see Chapter 15) to the person doing the job in your firm. If you don't have such expertise within your company then you should take steps to see that the individual concerned is helped to acquire the necessary knowledge and skills (eg, by reading appropriate books, by spending time with specialists from outside the firm – say, from a local business school or marketing consultancy). You may be able to get some advice from your trade association. If you engage the services of consultants, make sure that you get value for money and that they know what they are talking about.

There may be an appropriate short course available. If this area is particularly crucial for you, it may be useful for the person concerned to take a course at a college, or for you to recruit someone with the appropriate qualifications. Remember, however, that someone who is qualified still has to learn about the needs peculiar to your business to become fully effective.

SALES SUPPORT

If your promotional and sales activity is effective and results in a demand for your goods and services, you must have a way to respond positively and promptly. Who receives the orders and processes them? Who ensures that goods are despatched quickly, correctly packed and correctly labelled? Who records these actions for accounting and stock control purposes? Write down a set of questions like these which are appropriate to your firm – the few minutes it takes could prove to be time well spent. Asking these questions may help you tighten up the way orders are followed through, but our concern here is with the competence of all the people in the chain. Do they know what to do, what to record, and how their actions relate to what other people do? Do they recognize the significance of the action they take?

This need for support is particularly acute if you have some salespeople who move around a good deal and, hence, do not spend much time on the firm's premises. They feel particularly let down if their enquiries are not dealt with promptly, and if action does not follow swiftly when they send in orders. Never let the people in the office regard your salespeople as a 'nuisance'. They must be recognized as the 'front-line troops' and warmly supported. It often helps if they each have to deal mainly with just one person back at 'base', the firm's headquarters.

Sound training goes beyond enabling people to carry out routine tasks. It is also concerned with helping them understand why these tasks are necessary and how they fit into the overall picture. By taking this broader view of training, your people will be able to adapt more readily to changes in work patterns and procedures, and to respond sensibly to unforeseen events. This need for people to understand how their jobs match into the overall process is particularly important when their work is interdependent – as is processing orders, maintaining stocks and issuing invoices.

If your organization operates a delivery service, then route planning and the optimum stacking of goods in your vans may be an important cost factor in terms of both motor fuel and staff time. If you run a fleet of cars or vans, even a small one, then the optimum financial arrangements (eg, in terms of leasing or purchasing) can make an important impact on your profitability, cash availability and cash flow. Do you have people with the expertise to make these decisions?

COMPANY IMAGE

Some of your people are in the 'front line', dealing person to person with customers. They might be sales assistants, telephone salespeople, service engineers, craftsmen (eg, building contractors), estimators, and so forth. What sort of image do they present to potential or actual customers? Is it one of quiet efficiency, quality and concern with customer satisfaction? Or do your staff give the impression that customers are a necessary nuisance, to be endured to keep the business going? Or are customers regarded with complete indifference?

Don't be too hasty in your assessment. How do you know what image is projected? The 'customer as nuisance' image is by no means unknown. Once this question has been asked, the need to keep close to the customers and to ensure that your staff see themselves as there to meet the customers' needs is obvious. How do you do it? Remember that when it comes to staff attitude there are two key factors. First, your own attitude – if that is wrong then there's not much virtue in trying to make your staff see the need to cultivate customer satisfaction. Second, attitudes like this must be constantly reinforced. It is not something you do once, through a crash training course for example. You might have a pep talk and a discussion to start this off; but if you want to keep your staff keen, the way to do it is not to lecture to them, but to involve them in talking about it in a positive way. Ask them to chat over ideas on how you can improve the company image, the services you give to customers and the quality of your products. The more *you* are seen to be interested in this, the more your people will become interested.

These chats about customers should become a way of life. Hardly a day should go by without some comment being passed by you or your senior colleagues concerning quality, the customers or the need to maintain sales. This is not about formal meetings or training sessions, but about the ordinary conversations in the workplace on a day-to-day basis. This is where a lot of learning takes place.

This matter of image is not just for the front-line salespeople. It concerns everybody who has a contribution to make to the quality of your goods and services. It concerns everybody who has contact with the 'outside' world: people who write letters, answer the telephone or package your products. Have you ever telephoned your company incognito to find out how your telephone operator deals with the casual caller? You might get a pleasant surprise – or a nasty shock.

SKILLS NEEDED

You will see that we are building up an inventory of the knowledge and skills needed by people in your organization if marketing and selling are to be done effectively. It is up to you to see that the appropriate people have these skills. As we have seen, much can be done by coaching and by sparking off the right kinds of discussion and collaboration between people, but there may be some skills (like route planning, product specification, selling) where more formal courses can play a cost-effective part in improving your success.

ACTION GUIDELINES

1. Use the Marketing and sales checklist (Figure 1) to start you thinking about improving your product/services range and the effectiveness of your sales efforts.
2. Decide how you will gather information about your customers and their requirements, and about your competitors. If necessary, train your people to undertake this work.
3. Decide how you can use this market intelligence, and make sure your people are trained to capitalize on it.
4. Identify the key people in your sales effort and decide how you will maintain/increase their effectiveness.

5. Draw up your own checklists along the lines of the examples given (in Figures 2 to 6). Encourage your people to use them to ensure that every member of staff is fully competent to undertake his or her job.
6. Ensure that sales targets are used to motivate and develop your staff, as well as forming part of your management system.
7. Ensure that your salespeople get the support they need from other staff trained to recognize the importance of the rapid follow-up of orders and sales queries.
8. Stand back and consider the image your people present to the public, and in particular to your customers. If you are not happy with this image, set about training people to recognize where they have an impact on customers, and to impress them with the courtesy and efficiency of your firm.

CHAPTER 3

BUSINESS PLANNING

Although you might well be able to muddle along for some time without knowing exactly where all the money is coming from, or precisely where it is being spent, this is hardly a recipe for success. You need a business plan which gives an estimate of the cash you will require, and when, and how much this is likely to cost; and alongside this an estimate of what you can expect to sell, and when the income from sales is likely to materialize in your bank account. This will certainly be needed if you intend to raise cash from outside the firm.

Furthermore, you will want to introduce and maintain ways to keep an eye on how these estimates are working out in practice. It will be some kind of miracle if they work out as you expect, but hopefully your estimates will be of the right order of magnitude. You need to know quickly, and reliably, if things are not working out as you expected so that your plans can be modified in the light of your experience, and of changes in the market-place.

Remember that a business plan is a statement of expectation and intent; a basis for decisions; a tool to be used and adjusted in the interest of the business. It is not a blueprint to be slavishly followed come what may. In fact the *process* of planning is far more important than the final plan. The process imposes a valuable discipline which should ensure that you know what you are doing, what you are trying to achieve, and the kind of problems you might face.

WHO IS INVOLVED?

In any organization, it is the top man or woman who must take responsibility for the business plan, taking advice from specialists as appropriate. If these plans are to be soundly drawn up, people responsible for the key functions of the firm must be involved. In this connection it is useful to consider the main features of the business plan and who in the firm is responsible for contributing the information required or for making or sharing in the relevant decisions. Refer to the 'business plan checklist' in Figure 7.

Figure 7 Business plan checklist

What are the key features of the business, and the business plan? Who works with you on these and what skills do they need?

Have you drawn up the marketing and sales plan, and estimated when income from sales will accrue to the firm? Who assists you and what knowledge and skills do they require? (See Chapter 2.)

Have you agreed a timetable for each of the key decision points? Who was involved? Do they have all the skills they require?

When next you need more cash for investment, which of your people will assist you in deciding how to raise this? What knowledge and skills do they need?

Who negotiates the terms of important business agreements? Are they skilled at negotiation?

How is information gathered on sales made and income received; on costs incurred and expenditure levels? Are all the people involved fully competent to do this? (See Chapter 4.)

With whom do you discuss action to be taken in response to information about sales, supplies, and so forth? What skills do such people need to make a real contribution to good decisions?

WHAT IS YOUR BUSINESS?

When you first considered forming or taking over the company you now manage, you probably thought of the business in terms of the product or services which the company provided at the time. As time goes by you may wish to expand the company in terms of the range of products or services it provides or the customers it serves.

It often pays to take a step back and think about the business a little more deeply, and expand your own view as to its nature. It is wise to develop the firm in a way that makes sense in the market-place and in areas where you and your key people have expertise. It is prudent to talk through your business ideas with your senior people. Recognize that talking through your business with your senior staff as you prepare the plan is an excellent way to learn planning skills together. This also helps to build understanding and a team spirit, as each person realizes the part he or she has to play in relation to the roles and activities of others to make the business successful.

If you decide to move into areas where you don't have experience, you need to develop the knowledge and skills of someone in the firm, or to recruit someone from outside. You yourself cannot afford to remain completely ignorant of the new field, and you must take steps to ensure that you know the rudiments at the very least – if your own staff, or the people with whom you deal, suspect that you are ignorant of this aspect of the business, you could be heading for trouble.

In considering the nature of the business in relation to the market-place, there is merit in having an integrated approach. If you are making plastic mouldings for boats, for example, you could extend into making plastic mouldings for domestic furniture. In production terms this makes sense. This means you regard yourself as in the 'plastic mouldings' business. The problem is that you may have to go out and identify a completely new market, as the firms who buy plastic mouldings for boats may not want to buy items for domestic furniture.

An alternative strategy is to consider what other items you might make for boats. This would mean that you regard your firm as in the business of supplying materials for boat manufacture and the chandlery business. In either case you have a way of defining your business that makes sense, but the decision depends on a lot of careful thinking and discussions with your key people about the strengths and weaknesses of your firm, especially in terms of what it can supply, and about how readily you can gain access to different types of customer.

MARKETING PROGRAMME

The basic elements of the marketing and sales plan are outlined in Chapter 2. These elements need to be put down in an orderly framework and, together with your senior people, you need to look ahead and estimate what goods and services are likely to be sold, and when, and when the customers are likely to pay. The plan will also need to show what steps will be taken to advertise the firm's wares, how much this will cost, when the copy, etc will be needed, and when the bills will need to be paid.

Planning here will also involve making estimates of the effect of possible deviations from expectations, such as advertising not appearing on time (eg, because of newspaper strikes, postal delays), sales not meeting targets, some customers not paying bills promptly. Such data will be needed in the overall calculation of predicted cash flows and possible problems, such as cash shortfalls. Such planning may well involve thinking about contingency plans for unexpectedly high levels of sales. How soon can production be geared up to meet unexpected demand? Under what circumstances is extra advertising likely to prove worthwhile? What sums of money should be allowed for in the overall budget for this kind of thing?

Before any marketing plan can be implemented, some way of monitoring progress and recording and summarizing sales at intervals is required. Decisions will need to be made in the light of that information. Methods for achieving this should be agreed with the people concerned and specified in the plan.

How do people develop the skills of planning in marketing and sales? Books, and discussions in syndicates at business school courses and in business clubs can help to sharpen the mind, but in the smaller firm there is probably no real substitute for discussions on these matters among senior people and the salespeople. This should not be a generalized discussion, but focused on the firm's plans and the real problems you face together in bringing them to fruition.

ACTION TIMETABLE

The complexity of your timetable for decisions depends on how complicated your operations are in practice, and the stage of development of your firm. You may be able to answer all these questions on one side of a sheet of A4 paper. But if there are some crucial decisions where timing is important, you may find it useful to use critical path analysis.

For larger firms with more complex systems of organization, systems analysis techniques may be needed to help you get a grip on what is happening. Bear in mind that if you get in equipment or hire staff much before you can make proper use of them, or if you borrow a large sum of money before you need to spend it, you are incurring recurrent costs that will eat into your business. A little time spent in sensible planning could be a sound investment.

Critical path analysis and systems analysis techniques are not as complicated as they sound, and if you have not used them before but think they might be useful, don't hesitate to find out about them. The ability to use such methods should prove invaluable in the long run.

INVESTMENT STRATEGY

Raising capital for the business is now a complicated matter, and you will probably need to seek outside advice (eg, from your accountant) on the best way of achieving this. Bear in mind, however, that you have to make the decision and you have to bear the consequences. However good the advice, you should take the time to understand what is being suggested, and to think through the alternatives and their likely effect in the longer term.

If you think you need to improve your knowledge of these matters, you may, for example, be able to persuade your accountant or bank manager to spend a little time explaining them to you. Prepare for such a meeting by making a list of the items and terms you do not fully understand, and raise these as specific questions at the interview. This will ensure that you get value from the discussion. From time to time, short courses or seminars are arranged on such matters and you may find it useful to attend one of these.

NEGOTIATED AGREEMENTS

Are you confident that you and your staff are getting the best deals when you negotiate with the bank manager (for a loan), or with your suppliers (for credit, discount prices and delivery schedules), or with your larger customers (for a satisfactory price and reasonably prompt payment)? Successful negotiation depends on three things: starting from a position of reasonable strength; carefully preparing the ground before you start; and conducting the interpersonal relationships and interactions effectively. Thus, the competence of the people conducting the negotiations can often make a big difference to the outcome. Neglecting negotiating skills is rarely good business.

Generally speaking, the negotiator can do little about the starting position, although beginning with a begging bowl is not a good stance. It may be possible to diminish the effect of a weak position by considering carefully the basis of the deal in the preparation phase. If you can so arrange matters that what is advantageous for you is also advantageous for the other person, this helps, but it is not always possible. (See the notes on preparing for negotiation in *How to Manage People*.)

Whereas it is possible to learn something about preparing for negotiations from a book, the requisite interpersonal skills can be developed only through practice and reflecting on what happened in each case so that you can be more effective next time. There are some useful courses on negotiating skills to get you started. There are also packs available which will enable you to run a course yourself, but you must involve someone who has experience of interpersonal skills training, or someone who, at the very least, is sensitive to interpersonal behaviour.

If you consider that the quality of deals you are getting is adequate, there is no need to spend time on negotiating skills training. It may still be worth spending some time on careful preparation, however, as this may reveal ways of improving deals still further, especially in more complex cases.

CONTROLLING INFORMATION

When you have got a clear idea of the business you are in; what you hope to achieve; how you will assemble all the resources you will need to carry through your plans; the timing of key decisions; and the main elements in the key deals, you have a business plan. Remember that a business plan is not a set of tramlines along which you are now compelled to travel, but a route marked on a map, offering you one way to reach your destination, but not limiting you to that route. If the circumstances change, so must the action (route) you take. The plan must be updated, and adapted to changes.

This means that you need to know how things are going. Don't fall into the trap of trying to measure everything all the time and then finding that you can't handle all the data or that the cost of measuring is out of proportion to the results achieved. Decide what information is really important, where you can get it and how often you need it. Then make sure you have a system for achieving this, and that everyone who is involved in your system knows what is required, and when, and why.

Don't forget that, if information is to be reliable, it must be sound at the point of origin, and not distorted on the way. Where does the information start from? Do you have people filling out sales slips, completing forms, operating check-out tills which also give stock information, or making up lists? If those jobs are not done properly, your information is suspect. Time spent in training people to understand what they are doing and to complete documents correctly is essential. In such situations, people who understand the reasons for their tasks are more likely to cope with the unexpected, to notice peculiar data and to call attention to it, and to be prepared to suggest and to introduce modifications which will improve efficiency.

Every time information is transferred (eg, from one piece of paper to another, or into a computer, or in a telephone conversation) there is an opportunity for distortion and error. This means that your procedures should minimize such transfers. Get rid of every unnecessary piece of paper. Ensure that people check their own work when it is important, and feel responsible for its accuracy.

SKILLS NEEDED

From this discussion you can see the kinds of knowledge and skill needed if you are to have, and maintain, a sound business plan which will help you and your staff steer the firm. Make sure that your organization acquires these competences, and that as your firm grows, your ability to plan ahead grows as well.

Remember that involving your key people in the development of the plan has the twin advantages of helping to gain their commitment to the firm's objectives and giving them an understanding of the main issues involved. At the same time, it can provide an opportunity for the top team to learn together and develop the ability to work together more effectively.

Such involvement will also help when individual targets have to be set on a day-to-day basis, and when information for monitoring and control has to be collected. The real worth of the planning process will come to the fore when a crisis occurs and the plan has to be abandoned or modified severely. The information assembled for the plan and the insights gained will enable you to assess the impact of any new development, and to decide on how to deal with it.

ACTION GUIDELINES

1. Set out the key features of your business plan, and check it against the list in Figure 7.
2. If you do not have a business plan, consider with your key people the nature of your business and what realistic objectives can be set.
3. Agree a timetable for important decisions and how you will monitor progress.
4. Consider the crucial elements in your plan – marketing and sales, cash flow forecasts, critical deals, controlling information, etc – and decide how you will equip your key people to play their parts effectively, as well as gaining their commitment to success.

CHAPTER 4

Money Management

As far as money is concerned, the key to profitability and company survival lies in two simple ideas. First, the income generated must exceed the costs incurred. Second, the cash inflow into the company must occur in time to meet payments due. The management of money must ensure that both requirements are met; it is not good enough simply to show that the income due for goods and services provided during a given period exceeds the costs if that income is delayed beyond the point where pressing bills must be paid. *Cashflow*, as well as profit margins, must be predicted and monitored.

It is amazing how often the people who work in a firm have very little idea about how income is generated and where costs are incurred. People cannot be expected to collaborate in money management if they do not understand these things. If we are prepared to trust people, they are more likely to accept a measure of responsibility for the management of resources, and this can lead to an effective control system.

All this assumes, of course, that you have viable products and services and adequate markets for them, and that service to the customer is given the highest priority. In the short run, it may be expedient to offer some products or services at a loss for a short time to build up goodwill and to attract custom. Such action should be included in the planning and cash flow predictions. It is, in effect, an advertising cost. There may also be occasions when you help out a customer in need in ways that do not bring an adequate return at the time. But these specific and justified exceptions do not alter the need to monitor and control cashflow and profit margins, including the containment of costs. This can be accomplished effectively only with the whole-hearted support of a competent workforce.

The checklist in Figure 8 is designed to help you to identify some of the key steps in achieving the twin goals of profitability and a sound cash flow position, who is concerned with these goals in the firm, and what competences they require.

Figure 8 Managing money checklist

Who is involved in fixing the prices on each of your goods and services? What knowledge and skill do they require to do this work?

Who is involved in controlling costs? Are they aware of the cost factors? What relevant training have they received?

Who is involved in monitoring cashflow and in taking corrective action as required? Are they sufficiently trained/experienced to do this?

Are all your staff who are concerned with purchasing and supply aware of the need to contain costs of raw materials, etc, and of the importance of appropriate stock levels?

Are all your staff who are concerned with processing orders and customer invoices aware of the need for prompt efficient despatch of both goods and invoices, and of the need to follow up to ensure prompt payment?

Are all your managers aware of the basic management accounting systems in your organization, why they are needed and how they should be used?

Are employees at all levels:

- aware of cost/production targets?
- aware of the influence of quality and costs on sales?
- aware of the quality factors in their tasks?
- aware of the cost factors in their jobs?
- free to make cost-cutting suggestions?

COSTS AND PRICES

If your firm deals in only one commodity, sold in one size, and through one outlet, it is probably possible to allocate costs, including overheads, uniformly across the items sold to arrive at a cost per item. You must be careful to take into account periodic or sporadic payments, and tax liabilities. The difference between the selling price and your costs is the profit margin per item.

In most companies, however, there is a variety of products and/or services and a multiplicity of outlets and customers. Products are often sold in packs of different quantities. In such firms it is usually difficult to determine precisely the costs per item. In practice, this means that fixing competitive prices that bring in a profit is not as easy as it may seem. These calculations require skill and you need to ensure that you have people who can cope with these matters.

A close examination may reveal that some items are far more profitable than others, in purely financial terms. You may consider, however, that keeping less profitable items in your range of products helps you sell the others. You may also find that the lines with a lower profit margin per item sell more, and provide your stable baseline, making a satisfactory contribution to your overall profit. The question is, do you have the information available to make such decisions?

Are you confident that every item or service you sell is making its proper contribution, in one way or another, to the firm's profitability? These decisions are not a once-for-all matter, and it is important that people in your organization are trained to consider these issues regularly, and that they are capable of making sound recommendations to you based on the appropriate calculations.

There are a number of ways of deciding on the price you charge for goods and services, and also the amount of discount and credit you are prepared to allow to customers. A detailed discussion of these methods is outside the scope of this book, but the key point to bear in mind is that, overall, your prices must not be higher than the market will bear, or so low that you don't make a profit. If the market will bear a higher price for one or more of your products, so be it – there is no merit in sticking to a simple cost-plus formula in such cases.

On the other hand, you may be prepared to make a modest loss on a certain item for a period because of its prestige and advertising value. The important consideration here is, do you know just how much you could lose, and do you consider the value of the advertising justified?

These considerations show that pricing policy needs to be undertaken carefully and competently.

COST POLICY

A discussion of all costs arising in a business is, again, outside the scope of this book, but it is important that your senior staff understand your policy on this matter.

By way of illustration, consider an over-simplified picture of a manufacturing operation. Costs arise in the purchase and storage of raw materials, in fashioning the product and in storing the finished goods. The usual approach in Britain is to minimize production costs, and to bear the costs of storage of ample raw materials and finished goods to act as a buffer against fluctuating demand. An alternative approach is to minimize the stock of finished goods and invest in efficient plant which can match fluctuations in demand. Although the machines may lie idle or be just ticking over when not required, this can be cost-effective if, for example, the cost of storage of the finished goods is very high.

Another illustration is concerned with the use of machinery. Most firms work eight hours a day, five days a week, which means that machinery is lying idle for much of the time. Some firms work the machinery almost 24 hours a day, seven days a week, with highly-paid workers doing shiftwork.

On the retail side, some firms reckon to sell a few items at a very high mark-up price, while others expect to sell a large number of items at a low profit margin. Both strategies are effective, but the implications for the way costs are incurred are different. The first firm may consider it justified to invest in plush showrooms in fashionable areas, while the second might have a site in a busy shopping centre with spartan decor.

COST CONTROL

Profitability depends upon pricing policy, as we have seen, but the soundness of that policy depends on containing costs, especially overheads. Expenditure on general items like telephone bills, staff time, accommodation costs, machinery costs and maintenance contracts is not readily linked with particular items of output, and can easily escalate.

Since cost control depends, in large measure, on the day-to-day activity of managers and supervisors, it is important to ensure that they understand the facts of life about costs. Do they know the difference between fixed and variable costs – not just in general terms, but in terms of the processes, machinery and activities for which they are responsible? Do they know how much it costs to have a machine or a craftsman standing idle for an hour? Do they recognize that the same cost is incurred when the craftsman does an unnecessary task?

One way of improving cost-consciousness is to train your managers by getting them to calculate for themselves some of these costs. If you help them to get the requisite information and to do the calculations, they will learn not only about costs, but about sources of information within the firm. They might, later on, make use of these sources of information in other ways. Remember that it is not just the particular costs that matter: you are also creating a new way of looking at the jobs the managers do. You are, in effect, helping them see that they have a responsibility to *understand* the cost factors in the operation they manage and to take decisions accordingly.

Do they know the costs of raw materials, and hence what is lost when they are wasted through poor workmanship or incorrectly adjusted machines? Cost control is, generally speaking, much more effective if decisions are taken at the workplace, rather than by 'passing the figures up to the office' for someone else to notice that all is not right. Managers and supervisors should be encouraged to share their knowledge of where unnecessary costs arise, so that the workforce can help to keep these to a minimum.

Do those of your managers concerned with stock control know how much it costs in interest charges to maintain stocks at a higher level than necessary? Do those managers concerned recognize how easy it is to waste that often invisible but expensive raw material, fuel? Do those managers concerned with vehicles know how much it costs to keep them on the road, and how much money can be saved by efficient loading and route planning? (Such factors must, however, be subject to the overriding need to give a good service to your customers. It is false economy to keep stocks so low that you cannot meet customer demand promptly: the loss of an important customer could be a serious blow to the firm.)

It may, for example, be necessary to reset a machine several times to produce a range of goods each week to satisfy your customer's needs, whereas the efficient use of the machine would be to make the same item for a whole week. The customer comes first. In this case there may be another way: to build up stocks; but you must then consider whether you are assured of a market for the material stored, and you must also consider the costs incurred in storage space and the cost of the capital employed. Once again, the thinking behind such decisions should be shared with the managers concerned so that they understand what is going on and can play their full part in making the policy work. This is all part of the on-the-job coaching referred to in Chapter 15.

These considerations make it clear that training and developing the competence of your staff to control costs involves rather more than training them to observe efficient procedures. It is a matter of instilling into your managers and supervisors, and through them into the workforce as a whole, an appreciation of where costs arise, and how they can be contained without detriment to the quality of the goods and services you provide.

This can best be achieved through discussions, training and exploratory projects which enable managers and supervisors to understand costs within their own sections and how these relate to the prices of the finished products and services. In some cases you may want to send some of your staff on courses where the basic principles of management accounting are covered, but the knowledge so acquired needs to be supplemented and translated into the realities of your workplace and activities.

Don't be tempted to institute a lot of silly rules to contain costs. People resent crude attempts at controlling them, and may get a lot of enjoyment out of bucking the systems you introduce. Instead, channel their energies into helping you to run an efficient firm where their jobs will be secure and their income good.

CASH FLOW

Even if you have negotiated credit facilities with your suppliers, contained your outgoings on capital items, and sent out your invoices to customers promptly, the likelihood is that bills will come in faster than payments. Have you calculated how large this shortfall of funds could be, and when it could occur? Do you have a carefully prepared cash flow forecast? In practice, how will you know that this is about to happen, and how much notice will you have? How will you meet this crisis?

One way of reducing the danger of a cash shortage is to identify which bills are likely to be outstanding and significant, and then train your staff to bring legitimate pressure to bear on the debtors concerned to remit payment within a reasonable period. (This assumes that you already offer an incentive for early payment in the form of a discount if you anticipate that a number of purchasers might delay payment.

If a shortfall in income is virtually unavoidable, one way of preparing for the crisis is to have capital available on deposit, and another is to have an agreement with the bank on overdraft facilities. Either way you will need to know *before the crunch comes*. Quite apart from this, if your current account fluctuates wildly, you may wish to find a way of putting your short-term surplus cash to work earning interest.

There are, therefore, several reasons for effectively monitoring your cash flow. Although this is primarily a matter for your finance staff, all such information systems depend ultimately on the quality of the information fed into them at the outset. Thus, the members of your staff who complete returns, record cash received, and so forth, must be properly trained to know what they must do, and why.

PURCHASING AND SUPPLY

How much do your people know about the sources of supply and how to search out new suppliers, if necessary, to meet the needs of the firm? Are they fully aware of the stock levels needed to ensure production targets, cost of storage (in terms of space and interest on capital employed) and delivery dates for key materials? Are they sufficiently aware of the quality requirements of the firm in relation to the cost of raw materials? Are they trained to take full account of factors such as price reductions for bulk orders, where these are available? Can they work out optimum stock levels on the basis of all this data?

Much of this can be taught on the job by the managers concerned. If you can identify the kind of things people should know about, why not produce a simple checklist to help ensure that the manager covers all the important points? If there are certain decisions that are taken frequently, and where the same basic argument or calculation is carried out, it might be possible to prepare a job aid in the form of simple steps or an algorithm.

What communications are there between salespeople,

production people and the purchasing and supply people to ensure that the latter are alerted to possible future requirements? The supply side of the business often consumes a large proportion of the income, and it is essential that the key people who operate here have the ability, as well as the motivation, to contain costs.

In Chapter 12 there are some ideas on how you can get people to collaborate to increase their effectiveness. In essence, the key is to get them to share their objectives, to see that they can 'win' only if they work together, and to understand the tasks, problems and needs of the other sections involved.

ORDERS AND INVOICES

Sometimes the paperwork side of the organization is seen as a kind of Cinderella function – a repetitive and unglamorous drudgery. But people must deal efficiently with paperwork connected with orders received, and issue correctly-presented invoices when work is completed, if a healthy cashflow is to be maintained. The need here is to maintain the motivation of the people concerned as well as to ensure their competence.

Procedures should be as simple as possible; people concerned need to be trained on how to implement them. Emphasize again the importance of dealing courteously and efficiently with customers, whether by letter or telephone. Coach people to write polite letters to customers who are slow in paying their bills. It is often just as effective to say to people, 'We assume that your failure to pay our last invoice on time is an oversight', as to demand money with menaces. The stern letter is occasionally called for, as is even more serious action, but this should be a last resort rather than your first reaction.

FINANCIAL AWARENESS

All managers, supervisors and employees should be aware of the fact that satisfying the customer is the first rule of success in business, and that this sometimes means taking action that is, in the short run, not cost-effective in strictly financial terms. A manager might, for example, hire a taxi to take a small item to a customer who needs it in a hurry. Actions of this kind represent an investment in goodwill; hopefully, they will lead to future profitable sales.

Apart from matters of this kind, every manager and supervisor should recognize the importance of the careful management of money, and of all the resources which are ultimately paid out of the firm's income: time, space, machinery, raw materials, fuel, and so forth.

How do you instill this cost-consciousness? It must start at the top: if *you* don't care, why should anyone else? Your example counts for a great deal. After this, people need to be made more aware of the cost of the resources they are using. Get supervisors to cost out particular items and discuss the results with their staff. For example, how much does it cost, per five minutes, to operate one of your machines? (Take into account the hours worked, the annual depreciation and the fuel consumed.)

As another example, how much does it cost to have a one-hour meeting of your senior people? Take their salaries, employment costs and overheads for the year and divide the total by the average number of hours worked, allowing for holidays and sickness. Then the next time you meet, you can say that you expect value for money from the meeting in view of its cost.

No doubt you can think up dozens of similar examples in your own firm. Choose one or two and get people to do the work so that they become gradually more aware of where money is spent. In many cases, like your meeting of senior people, you will not be able to evaluate the outcome simply in money terms, and must make a judgment of its worth. Getting people into the habit of making such judgments will be of real value to the firm. Another way of looking at this is to consider what decisions were made as a result of that meeting, and how crucial they were. (Of course, you can also assess the financial cost of making the wrong decision!)

Don't fall into the trap of measuring all sorts of costs because they are easy to measure. That is often a waste of time and money in itself. Be sure you measure and evaluate the things that really matter in terms of the effectiveness and profitability of the firm.

ACTION GUIDELINES

1. Emphasize and encourage income generation more than cost control, and consider the customer first.
2. Remember that cash flow is just as important as profitability.

3. Involve key people in pricing policy decisions and train them to appreciate the issues involved.
4. Encourage people to do their own cost controlling. Train your managers to understand where costs arise, and encourage a cost-conscious workforce. Don't install a lot of silly cost-saving rules.
5. Monitor your cash flow and take appropriate action. Prevent problems wherever possible by training people to secure prompt payment on the invoices you issue.
6. Make sure people recognize the significance of financial factors and feel eager and competent to deal with them.
7. Ensure that sound money management is seen to start at the top.

CHAPTER 5

QUALITY ASSURANCE

Whatever kind of business you run, customers will make judgments about the quality of your goods and services, and also about the way in which you and your staff deal with their enquiries, orders and after-sales requirements. Such judgments will often have a decisive effect on whether or not these customers continue to do business with you, and whether they recommend you to other potential customers.

There is a lot of evidence to suggest that the way you and your people behave towards your customers is even more important than the quality of goods and services you provide. That does not mean that you can afford to neglect the quality of what you provide: what it means is that you must give, at the very least, equal priority to ensuring that your customers are made to feel welcome, supported and well-served by every member of your staff with whom they come into contact.

Notice the use of the word 'feel' in the sentence above. The way people 'feel' depends on their perceptions, on the way they see things. It has been said, with a lot of truth, that people buy from people they like. Do customers 'like' your people?

No doubt you have already worked out quality standards for your own products and services. The precise meaning of the term 'quality' will depend on the commodity in question: whether it is tangible objects; well-defined services; or services which are more complex to define, where it is difficult to prescribe standards. There are, however, ways of considering the quality of a specialist's advice, the attention of a sales assistant, the repair of a TV set, treatment by a dentist or the presentation and content of a training course.

Although setting quality standards is a highly technical

matter, specific to the kind of goods or service you are providing, there are some general principles which apply, in varying degrees, to every kind of quality assurance. If you are concerned with the manufacture of large numbers of similar items, there are well-known statistical techniques that may be useful to you – provided that a key quality feature in your product is susceptible to measurement.

In developing people to establish and maintain quality, you will need to ensure that:

- Your firm is sensitive to the customers' expectations, and ways in which these might change.
- Your staff are fully trained to recognize quality and to achieve this in their technical activity.
- Your staff are quality-conscious, and prepared to take action promptly to ensure that defective goods are not provided to customers, and that examples of poor service are quickly identified and rectified.
- All your staff are conscious of the importance of good customer relations in all their dealings and decisions.
- Your staff are trained to act as a team, sharing the quality aims and supporting each other to achieve them.

In the United Kingdom, the British Standards Institute has prepared a particular standard for those who wish to assure the quality of their goods and services, and many companies have adopted this procedure to provide added assurance to their customers.

CUSTOMER REQUIREMENTS

The starting point for quality standards is the customer. What is your source of intelligence about customer requirements? Which members of your staff are monitoring the kinds of customer who are buying your goods? How are these staff members being used? Which of your people is keeping in touch with the kinds of customer who use the services, and with their expectations? Bear in mind that although you may derive satisfaction from making articles of a certain kind of quality, if you are in business, it is the standard required by the *customers* that counts.

If you have not done your homework, it is possible that you may be emphasizing an aspect of quality that is not critical as far as your customers are concerned, and neglecting an aspect of real concern to them. A firm making computer cabinets once found its employees spending a lot of time buffing the inside of the cabinets, when only the removal of sharp edges from welded joints was required. The exterior finish and the precise location of drilled holes were far more important to the computer firm that purchased these cabinets.

QUALITY STANDARDS

Who is responsible for setting quality standards? Is the individual concerned fully conversant with any health and safety considerations, legislative requirements or publicly recognized quality standards (eg, British Standards)? You must ensure that the person concerned is not merely aware of these standards, but is able to keep up to date, and has the ability to understand these requirements and to interpret them in relation to your products and services.

If you are dealing with commodities where the handling and treatment involve considerable technical know-how and understanding (eg, with processed foodstuffs, chemicals, mechanical or electrical devices), particular care is needed in training the people who make decisions and handle the materials.

Once again, it is the customer who comes first. How does the person concerned with quality standards in your outfit know that these meet the customers' requirements? There is usually a trade-off between quality and costs – getting the balance right requires knowledge, skill and judgment. How do you ensure that those concerned acquire the knowledge, skill and judgment needed?

Technical knowledge, and skills in a general sense, can be obtained through appropriate courses and reading textbooks and periodicals, but this may need to be supplemented by on-the-job training and coaching, especially if your firm is at the forefront of technology. Do you positively encourage this on-the-job learning and coaching?

Knowledge of customer requirements is more difficult. Looking at customer needs is not generally a job for the quality-maintenance person, but this kind of information should be the touchstone for standards.

QUALITY MAINTENANCE

Ultimately, quality depends on workmanship, and as we have seen this depends on skill and motivation. The first step is to ensure that your staff have the ability to make the goods and provide the services at the required standard. Then you will need to enthuse them with the desire to make good quality products and to give good quality service.

Once again your own example can be very powerful. Your concern for quality, and your pride in running a company that produces quality products and services, will influence those who work for you. If you set up elaborate quality inspection procedures where one person 'checks' another person's work, you will be implying that you do not trust the original worker to do a good job.

Of course, this may be entirely justifiable where the worker is new and learning the ropes, and in some very critical areas it may be essential for two people to check every item. In general, however, it is best to arrange things so that people take responsibility for the quality of their own workmanship, either individually or in small groups. This means that such workers must be trained not only to do the original work, but to recognize the quality required and to carry out inspection and testing procedures on the goods they have produced. This has implications for any reward system you employ, which must be consistent with the quality standards you require and must encourage people to maintain these standards.

Maintaining quality means attention to detail at each stage, including initial inspection of raw materials, machine settings, manufacture, packaging, distribution and display. If you want people in your firm to maintain vigilance at this kind of level, you need to keep up the momentum. Attitudes can easily become lax, especially if there appears to be a falling off of enthusiasm at the 'top' of the firm.

There are some kinds of operation where measured standards of quality and the results of prescribed tests at each stage must be recorded in some way – this is particularly the case in the aircraft industry, and in some aspects of food manufacture, for example. You will need to ensure that proper procedures are put in place and maintained.

In the case of retailing and catering activities, quality refers not only to the goods provided, but also to the environment, to 'good housekeeping', cleanliness and tidiness, and to the efficiency and courtesy of the service. Training people in these areas is of prime importance.

The importance of 'service' is also relevant to manufacturing operations. Nowadays we should think of a manufacturing company as providing a service, part of which consists of the goods made. Examples of other components of the service include: promptness of delivery; information on how to choose and use the goods to their best effect; back-up supplies of materials and spares; and prompt, efficient help with maintenance and repairs.

REMOTE STAFF

It is not difficult to keep in touch with the quality of workmanship and service provided by people who work on the premises of your factory, laboratory, office or shop. It is more difficult to ensure that the people who work away from the site (eg, building craftsmen, carpet fitters, service engineers, sales representatives and delivery drivers) maintain your standards. Never forget that they are your front-line representatives. In many cases they are the firm as far as the customer is concerned. The impression they make, in terms of efficiency, courtesy and keenness to do a good job, is the impression your customers have of your business.

Many of the people who work away from the firm are not trained salespeople, but they may well spend more time in contact with your customers than your sales representatives do. This means that the training of such people should involve more than just the appropriate technical training (ie, training for bricklaying or electrical wiring, carpet fitting, machinery repair, or product knowledge and selling techniques, for example). The people concerned need to understand the style and standards of the firm, and be committed to maintaining these standards. This is a matter of both social skills (see Chapter 18) and attitudes (see Chapter 14).

TEAMWORK AND QUALITY

As we have seen, achieving quality in goods and services requires a combined effort involving many people. If you allocate responsibilities for different aspects of quality to different people, they may be less likely to pick up problems in other people's areas. The only answer to this is to ensure that people regard themselves as part of a team whose job is to ensure quality at all stages and at all levels.

They need to understand how quality is achieved at each stage and what to look for, so that when problems arise they know who to talk to and do so in a positive and constructive manner. You do not want people simply blaming each other or finding fault, but encouraging each other and supporting each other in maintaining quality and output cost-effectively. Hints on how to foster this kind of teamwork are provided in Chapter 12.

ACTION GUIDELINES

1. Identify and train those who are responsible for determining the customers' requirements in terms of quality.
2. Identify and train those who are responsible for setting quality standards for your goods and services, and ensure effective liaison with the people identified above.
3. Ensure that those who define the standards of workmanship necessary to achieve this quality understand the reasons for the quality standards as well as how they can be achieved in practice.
4. Identify and train those responsible for checking the quality of incoming goods and materials and for quality checks at intermediate stages of manufacture (where necessary).
5. Place those people responsible for ensuring quality as close as possible to those who make the products or provide the services, and train and motivate them to achieve the standards necessary.
6. Take steps to ensure 'teamwork' (ie, that people share responsibility for producing quality goods and services, recognize the contribution each person makes, and know how to co-operate to achieve the desired results).

CHAPTER 6

Transport and Distribution

Storage and distribution costs form a high percentage of the purchase price of most products – 25 per cent is not uncommon. Training your people to control these costs by sound management and procedures makes good business sense. Apart from the straightforward problem of controlling packaging, storage and carriage costs, there is a need to minimize – and in some cases to avoid completely – losses through spoilage during storage and transit, and through pilferage. (However, if your firm is not involved to any extent in distribution problems, you can skip this chapter.)

DISTRIBUTION CHOICES

Your livelihood depends on satisfied customers, and it is the condition of your goods when they reach the customer that counts. Your staff will need to recognize that in storage and distribution there are three areas of trade-off: the cost, the speed and the quality of the goods on arrival. The priorities accorded to these factors will vary according to the nature of your business.

If you are making small, non-perishable items using expensive machinery, you will wish to maximize the hours during which the machinery is employed; and provided sales potential is good, you will be prepared to pay the modest storage costs of holding buffer stocks, and perhaps using slow and cheap methods of transportation. But if inexpensive machinery is being used to make items which are large or perishable (ie, must be stored under controlled conditions), you may wish to minimize storage costs, and to link the use of production capacity more closely to sales.

If your product is highly priced and not price-sensitive, you may be happy to pay high packaging and transportation costs to ensure that it reaches the customer quickly and in prime condition. On the other hand, if your product is bulky or the profit margin per item low, packaging and distribution costs must be closely controlled. Products which are dangerous, delicate or perishable must be adequately protected, and the costs of this must be borne in the pricing structure.

The location of storage facilities is also a key factor in terms of storage costs and transportation. For example, many high street shops are now moving many of their products to cheaper warehouse sites and bringing merchandise in as required to enable more of the expensive high street space to be used for the business of selling goods and display.

Someone in your firm must face up to these issues and ensure that your storage and distribution practices are appropriate to your products and the demands of the market. Does that person have the necessary knowledge and experience to make these decisions? Once taken, these decisions should be subject to periodic review as relative costs (eg, of storage space or of different forms of fuel) fluctuate, or as market requirements change.

OVERALL CONTROL

Assuming these decisions have been taken, someone must maintain an overview of what is happening in terms of packaging, storage and distribution. This should not be difficult in a small firm, but the person concerned needs to know enough about the subject to remain alert to ask the right questions about storage conditions, packaging quality and costs, the condition of vehicles, and so forth.

Wherever possible, it is useful to gain some feedback from your customers about the condition of your goods on arrival, promptness of delivery, correctness of paperwork and the make-up of the consignment. In general, proper control can be exercised only if the information system, whether computerized or entirely on paper, is well designed, easy to use and followed in practice. The person in control should understand this system thoroughly, and be able to interpret any unusual data or warning signal that arises.

Customer complaints should be promptly and thoroughly investigated. Don't look for scapegoats to take the blame; look for ways of preventing recurrence. Investigating complaints in this problem-solving way can be an excellent way of learning *together* how to improve company performance. The complaint may not be due to storage or distribution conditions, but to some difficulty with raw materials or in the manufacturing process; but the way to tackle it is still to use it as a source of lessons for the future.

PERISHABLE AND DANGEROUS GOODS

If you distribute dangerous or perishable commodities, whether packaged or not, it is important to ensure that everyone who handles these is fully convinced that the precautions to be taken are necessary (study Chapter 8 carefully). The precautions to be taken in packaging, transit and conditions of storage require specialist knowledge of the materials concerned and of any regulations regarding their handling, storage and transportation. Make sure you have people who know about these matters, or seek professional advice and see that key people are trained to understand what is involved. Make sure enough people are trained to cover for absences owing to holidays or sickness. If a query or problem should arise, you want authoritative answers double-quick, and appropriate action without delay.

CARRIAGE, DAMAGE AND LOSS

There are a number of hazards to goods in transit, and your staff will need to know which ones are significant in your trade and hence require special attention. Some goods in transit also offer a hazard to the people handling them, and to the general public. In such cases there will be regulations with which your firm will need to comply: your trade association will probably be able to keep you up to date with legal requirements and the appropriate precautions to be taken. All the staff concerned will need to be trained at the outset to handle goods carefully and safely, and be kept updated on any new requirements that emerge.

Exposure to weather will harm most products. Many products are harmed by rodents, bacteria and fungi. Some products need to be kept in temperature-controlled conditions – maybe in particular gaseous atmospheres. In general, the most serious risk for manufactured goods in transit is breakages of fragile products, which may be damaged by vibration, compression or impact.

Losses can also occur through theft, and if this is a significant problem in your business, your staff will need to have liaison with the police. You may need to provide special security training. You must also be prepared to face the possibility that your own staff may be involved in pilferage. The only way to handle such a problem is by building a sense of loyalty to the company by fair employment policies and treatment, coupled with sensible precautions so that employees know there is a high probability of detection.

Your staff will need to be trained to assess the likely causes of loss and to take precautions as appropriate, including insurance cover, bearing in mind that the cost of this cover is dependent on the value and the fragility of your goods. The relative merits of alternative forms of transportation for different products should also be considered.

Some companies find it necessary to employ sub-contractors to handle security matters, but this still leaves a need for someone with expertise in managing such contracts and contractors.

When goods are carried by the Post Office or other commercial carriers, your staff need to bear in mind the optimum size, weight, etc, and also the fact that often the packages will be roughly handled.

PACKAGING

Packaging is sometimes thought of as a Cinderella department, but if your goods are not packaged effectively and economically, your reputation will soon suffer. Indeed, in some industries, such as cosmetics, the packaging may be considered almost as important as the product.

If the goods are uniform in size and shape, an assembly-line procedure or a simple packing machine may be used. In many small firms, however, the products come in a variety of shapes and sizes, and often several items are included in a single pack for despatch. The training required here is concerned with versatility: the ability to take a variety of components and place them into packaging material and a covering envelope or carton without undue waste of packing materials or time. If the operations are at all complex, use the 'discovery method' of training outlined in Chapter 16.

Where the packaging is also used for merchandising or is part of the presentation of the goods (eg, to retail customers), extra precautions need to be taken to create and maintain its attractiveness.

VEHICLES

If your firm uses vehicles to transport goods, then the drivers and others concerned need to be trained in the proper care and maintenance of the vehicle itself, not only in relation to its roadworthiness, but also in relation to the goods to be carried. This training is in addition to the normal training for driving the vehicle. Where drivers must take their vehicles across international borders, there is a great deal of knowledge and skill to be acquired in dealing with the documentation and relevant regulations.

Vehicles which carry 'open' perishable foods need to be kept clean and hygienic. If refrigerated material is carried, then the driver will need to know how to operate and check the temperature control mechanism, and what action to take if this mechanism becomes defective.

Some van drivers are also involved in selling, and perhaps cash handling, as well as in loading and unloading goods and driving the vehicle. Bear in mind that in addition to product knowledge and cash handling skills, such people need to develop social skills.

ROUTE PLANNING AND TRANSPORT MANAGEMENT

If your transport operation involves a number of pick-up points and/or delivery venues, careful planning of the route to be taken can save costs. Do you have someone who can take into account the mileages involved in alternative routes, collection and delivery schedules, road conditions, customer preferences, restrictions on stopping outside particular premises, and so forth? If you have a complicated delivery system, you will probably find that there is a simple computer programme which can be used to help select the most cost-effective routes.

If transportation forms an important part of your business, you will need to ensure that someone within your organization is properly qualified to manage the operation and ensure that it is conducted efficiently, profitably and safely.

ACTION GUIDELINES

1. Who determines the distribution strategy for your firm and makes choices about costs, speed and the protection of your goods?
2. Who ensures that your goods reach the customer in the best condition possible?
3. Who ensures that all necessary precautions are taken in the packaging and distribution of perishable or dangerous goods? (Remember that there are rules governing the handling and transportation of dangerous and inflammable materials, hazardous loads and most perishable goods.)
4. Who packages goods for despatch from your company's premises?
5. Where the transportation is sub-contracted, who ensures that optimum load sizes are used?
6. Where transportation is by sea or air, who ensures that the best route and method are employed, and that packaging is appropriate?
7. If you distribute with your own vehicles, who loads vans and lorries with your goods?
8. Who ensures that all your vehicles are maintained in a presentable and roadworthy condition?
9. Who plans and optimizes the routes taken by your vehicles?
10. Are you confident that the staff in charge of all above tasks are fully competent to carry out their duties?

CHAPTER 7

MANAGING INFORMATION

Whatever kind of outfit you run, you must handle information – about purchases, sales stocks, people employed, money transfers, statutory returns, etc. If this information is not handled correctly and promptly at every stage, you will run into trouble, and that could be costly. Inefficiency in the way information is handled can lose orders, delay income and cause problems with government departments.

In larger firms, there may be several offices which process information, each dealing with a different aspect of the business, such as sales, purchasing or transport. In a smaller firm, all these functions are generally contained within one room – the general office – but as computers and word processors become more widespread, this concept of an office is likely to change. Instead of a central point through which all the information passes, we shall have a network of computer terminals where information is fed in and drawn out as it is needed: at the check-out till, at the telephone sales desk, in the material store room and in the packing department, for example. The boss will have a terminal on his or her desk as well.

At present, however, we are concerned with what information has to be handled and who deals with it; whether this is done in a separate room called an office, or by several people scattered around the firm.

One way of finding out who will need training in managing information is to trace the key pieces of information: where they come from; how they are used; what decisions are made and what action is taken based upon them; and who is involved. This is a lengthy process and worth undertaking only if you consider you have serious problems (eg, insufficient information for sound decisions, or an information overload). If you have a specific information-handling problem (eg, if you consider that the method of processing orders is too slow), then this type of analysis is worthwhile.

AN INFORMATION SYSTEM

In simple terms, an information system has three basic steps. First, the information gets into the system. Second, the information is processed in some way, often in combination with other data. Third, the information is presented to the user, and often decisions have to be made based on this information. For example, the telephone rings, and a customer requests a consignment of ribbon. Information is entering the system. The processing should begin immediately.

The clerk who answers the telephone may request the name and telephone number of the client, then refer to a video screen to check on the availability of the material required, and confirm that it is available. Then the price and probable delivery date are quoted, the order is confirmed and the address and account number of the client are taken. All this information is fed into the system (correctly we hope!). The order is then passed through the system until the consignment of ribbon is despatched (action based on the information). Lastly, combined with data about the price of the goods and any discount due, the information is used to prepare and despatch the invoice.

If there is a possibility that delivery of the goods or their condition may be questioned, then there may be a need for the customer to sign a copy of the delivery note which is then returned to the company to be matched up with the other documents. In cases where payment is in dispute, three associated documents need to be produced – proof of order, proof of delivery and the invoice.

Such information-handling events occur everyday in many firms, but this sequence provides plenty of opportunities for errors (eg, when the information is first recorded, when it is processed and calculations are involved, and when it is interpreted and used for making a decision). What is worse, it is sometimes easy for errors to go undetected for some time, with consequent losses to the firm. Apart from this, processing information is expensive, and it is easy for those concerned to waste time and money through inefficiency, even when the overall operation does not seem to be impaired. Incompetent information-handling can have a direct effect on customers and suppliers, who may form a poor impression of your firm if telephone calls and correspondence are slipshod.

IMPROVING INFORMATION HANDLING

How can you make a start to tighten up and improve your office work? The first step is to take a broad look at what you need to achieve in this area. One way is to work through the 'action guidelines' at the end of this chapter. Don't do this on your own: bring into the discussion the people doing the job and the people who need to use information in your firm. These discussions are part of training and learning (see Chapter 15). You will thus gain a better understanding of what is involved at ground level, and your people will get a better grasp of who needs the information they deal with, and why.

One way in which a great deal of time and money can be wasted is in having too much information floating about – bits of paper that nobody really needs but that somebody requested at some time in the past. It is worth asking, from time to time, who needs this information and why.

Another simple way to look at improvements in office efficiency is to examine each of the jobs people do at present and, using the checklist in Figure 9 (on page 54), decide which skills these people need. In some cases (eg, where skills like using a keyboard are involved) it will be cost-effective to train the person concerned away from the workplace, but in many instances the skills and knowledge required are best attained on the job, where the supervisor can show the individual how to perform the requisite task. In the case of comparatively simple machines like copiers, the simple instructions printed on the machine or supplied by the manufacturer can be used as job aids with very little instruction.

Where such job aids are used, care should be taken to emphasize any danger points and precautions to be taken. Both the safety angle and any possible damage to the machine must be taken into account. On-the-job training is usually best where there are simple procedures to be learned which are specific to the company.

MANAGING RELATIONSHIPS

Generally speaking, the office is essentially an aid to the

business, and it does not generate income in itself. But the possession of information can give people a sense of power and can cause strained relationships between office personnel and others, such as van drivers, production workers or sales representatives. If you detect this, it may be necessary for you or your senior staff to encourage people to recognize that they are all part of a team that must work together and understand each others' concerns if the firm is to prosper. Strains of this kind often arise when people do not understand the roles of others, and the part they each have to play in bringing about the success of the enterprise.

One way to help prevent this kind of misunderstanding is to ensure that, as part of their induction, newcomers spend a little time finding out about the work of the people they will relate to in their own work. Where the misunderstanding has arisen, it may be worthwhile having a careful structured discussion where the people involved explain, in simple terms, what their work is, what information they receive and what information they need to be effective.

If you decide to mount such a session, keep it short – no more than an hour. Make sure people look towards real operational matters and how to improve them. Don't allow this to become a session where everybody just moans about their problems. If an hour proves to be too short, do not rush through the discussion, but arrange another one-hour session later. The secret of success in such sessions is to focus on the future and how to improve communication and performance. It is not helpful to dwell for long on the problems which have arisen, except as indicators of the need for change. Above all, look for solutions to problems, not scapegoats.

Figure 9 Office skills checklist

Written work Write clearly and neatly. Record or transcribe information in words accurately. Follow written instructions. Convert spoken information into written information. Compose brief but explicit messages. Compose business letters. Write reports. Complete forms correctly. Draw charts or graphs. Read technical drawings. Take shorthand dictation.

Use of information Understand and use information

received. Extract relevant information from documents. Use tables of information correctly.

Numerical work Add and subtract in money. Add and subtract in measures. Multiply and divide in money. Multiply and divide in measures. Work with decimals. Work with fractions. Work with percentages. Count and check cash accurately.

In conversation Converse with people to give and receive information. Conduct telephone conversations to give and receive information. Follow oral instructions clearly. Present a point of view persuasively. Instruct someone in how to perform a task.

Checking Check documents for completeness. Check that calculations/estimates are correct. Compare records and documents for discrepancies. Proof read against original. Scan figures to detect illogicalities or errors.

Sorting/filing Sort items into correct order (sequences or groups). Index items. Cross-reference items. Alphabetical filing and retrieval. Numeric filing and retrieval. Collate documents.

Keyboard skills Type accurately, neatly and quickly. Type letters, reports and forms. Type tables and figures. Use a computer/word processor.

Office machinery Able to use relevant office machinery (eg, telephone, adding machine, addressing machine, telephone switchboard, postal franking machine, dictating machine, typewriter, printer for word processor/computer, guillotine, copier, binding machine).

Miscellaneous Follow prescribed procedures. Plan own work. Work without supervision. Seek advice when necessary. Respond to urgency. Tact in dealing with others. Act as a receptionist. Negotiate with suppliers and/or customers. Maintain confidentiality of information.

Such a modest investment in time should be amply repaid in fewer misunderstandings and mistakes, with all the associated costs (in time and money) involved in re-doing jobs and rectifying errors.

THE TELEPHONE AS AN ASSET

The telephone is now a virtually inescapable component of business activity where information has to flow. But the telephone is like any other inanimate object: it can be used for the good of the firm, or it can be misused. The telephone bill is probably a significant factor in your current expenditure. You should make sure you get value for money here, as elsewhere in the business. Making good use of the telephone depends essentially on two things – being clear about how the telephone can help the business; and making sure all your people know how to use it efficiently.

Knowing how to use the telephone properly in business is more than simply knowing which end to talk into and how to dial a number. Think of some of the ways in which the telephone is used in your firm. Before you read on, jot down a brief list of, say, four or five ways in which the telephone can be helpful to your outfit.

What kind of item is on your list? Essentially, the telephone is a means of communication, and thus it can be used, for example, for selling, purchasing, cultivating contacts, image-building, dealing with queries or providing a service. These activities are, of course, not mutually exclusive. An image, for good or ill, is created in every telephone call. Cultivated contacts may lead to profitable sales or sound purchases in due course.

Unfortunately, if wrongly used, the telephone call can also hinder the firm in each of these areas. Furthermore, abuse can result in very high telephone charges. If telephone calls are profitable, fine – if not, you have a problem. You should ensure that staff know about different charging rates at different times of the day.

Image building

The response people get whenever they telephone your firm helps to create an image of what the firm is like. If they are answered by irascible staff who seem to regard them as a nuisance on the telephone – and this can and does happen – they get the message that the firm does not care about its customers or business associates. Everyone who answers the telephone needs to recognize this, and to respond quickly, courteously and efficiently to incoming calls. It is important that the caller is made to feel welcome, and is quickly transferred to the relevant person.

All this seems pretty obvious, but it is amazing how offhand, and sometimes even off-putting, the company telephone operator (and other people in the firm) can seem. The customer caller is important, and probably regards his or her time as important, but it is not uncommon for telephone operators to leave callers in 'mid air', while they mess about trying to contact the appropriate department. A courteous, considerate and efficient operator can do a lot to encourage callers to have confidence in the firm, and customers to make purchases.

If your firm sells by telephone, you should seriously consider arranging formal off-the-job training for both the telephone salespeople (see Figure 6) and the telephone operator (see Figure 10).

Telephone your own company occasionally without saying who you are, so that you can gain some impression of how the firm deals with callers. If all is well, fine. If not, consider carefully the notion of drawing up simple 'company guidelines' on the use of the telephone. Don't do this on your own: get some of your staff together, especially the ones who use the telephone a lot. Ask them to draft some guidelines, or draw them up together.

The draft provided in Figure 10 is intended to stimulate thought, not to be obeyed to the letter as it stands. Remember that people learn when they get involved in projects of this kind. It's a form of training to get people to draw up the guidelines. What is more, people tend to use guidelines they have drawn up for themselves more readily than ones which are given to them without discussion.

Figure 10 Telephone operator checklist

The telephone operator must be able to:

Speak clearly and concisely on the telephone
Respond in a constructive and helpful manner to callers
Operate the telephone equipment quickly and competently

Find extension numbers quickly (eg, from internal directories)
Answer minor queries personally
Know enough about the firm to refer callers to appropriate members of staff where necessary
Follow the firm's guidelines on the use of the telephone
Transfer calls, keeping the caller informed at each stage
Maintain a cool and constructive attitude when problems arise or callers sound upset for any reason
Assess priorities when several demands surface simultaneously
Dial calls for members of staff, including overseas calls as required.

How formally you use these guidelines depends on the size and nature of the business. If your firm is very small and only two or three people ever use the telephone, there's no need to make a meal of it: you can just use Figure 10 as the basis of an occasional chat with the people concerned. If a lot of people use the telephone, you may need to do more to get the essential message across. Don't forget here, as in other cases, the importance of example. If you use the telephone in a 'slapdash' way, don't expect your staff to do otherwise.

Selling by telephone

There are two kinds of telephone selling. Your telephone number can be made known to your clients through advertising literature or personal contact, so that potential customers telephone the firm to enquire about your products and services, to place orders and to arrange visits. Alternatively, you may decide to compile a list of potential clients and get a member of your staff to telephone each one in turn to seek to make sales.

This subject has been mentioned in Chapter 2, where an indication of the training needs of telephone salespeople is given. If your firm sells by telephone, refer again to Chapter 2, and to Figure 6. Unless your salespeople have a separate telephone line (which may be useful if this is a major activity), the call may come to another member of staff or to the switchboard. As mentioned above, the potential customer should be made to feel welcome, and be transferred quickly to the salesperson concerned.

Buying by telephone

Much of your purchasing is probably done by mail, but often it is quicker and more efficient to use the telephone to place orders, especially where time is of the essence and your credit is good. There is probably no need for more than on-the-job training to ensure that those who do this work know how to use the telephone, and are careful about preparing to make calls and keeping proper records – as indicated in the firm's guidelines on telephone use (see Figure 10). This should be covered in the initial training for newcomers.

Cultivating contacts

In conducting any business there are a number of people with whom you need to keep in contact, apart from those involved with the formal placing of orders, etc. These contacts may include, for example, your bank manager and accountant, officials in the trade bodies with which you are associated, public bodies, potential suppliers or customers.

Some of these contacts may be maintained informally over lunch or at the local golf club, and again the telephone is invaluable for keeping contacts alive and arranging occasional meetings. The problem is deciding when to telephone and what subject to choose for discussion. Prolonged discussion about irrelevancies will hardly endear you to these contacts, so giving some thought to your strategy here can be worthwhile. This is not a matter for training courses, but it may be worth spending a little time discussing among your senior colleagues a cost-effective way of keeping in touch with key contacts, and the topics to choose for occasional telephone conversations.

Services by telephone

So far we have talked about the telephone as a means of conducting your business, but it can also be used to generate income in its own right. You might, for example, offer an information service for a subscription. Trade associations, professional bodies and research institutes can offer information services to their members, including a commitment to answer questions over the telephone. This service can be provided commercially if you have the expertise and information back-up in an area where people value such a service.

Some equipment manufacturers, notably in the computer field, offer a telephone back-up service to purchasers. If the purchaser has problems with the machine, a telephone conversation may solve the difficulty without the need for a visit from a service engineer. This is a commercial arrangement, where the price of this service is effectively included in the sale price of the machine. Similar arrangements can be made under service contracts.

Another example is where companies that specialize in the stock, commodity or futures markets undertake to provide an up-to-the-minute information and advisory service for clients over the telephone. The motoring organizations also provide information and advice over the telephone as part of their service to members.

Clearly, in every case the quality of the telephone conversation is crucial to success. Here, the preparation – in terms of having information at the fingertips of the people answering the telephone, and expert advice on call – is fundamental to success. Training the people concerned to retrieve that information and advice quickly and correctly must form an important part of the setting up and maintenance of such an operation.

Training needs

It is rarely necessary to provide formal off-the-job training in the use of the telephone (except in the case of the switchboard operator), although some form of training should be provided, if necessary, for newcomers or school-leavers. Informal training, based on the firm's guidelines (see Figure 11), should be the responsibility of managers and supervisors. (Note: Figure 11 is simply a guide and you should draw up your own checklist.)

Figure 11 Guidelines on using the telephone

When making a call:

Make sure you have the correct name and telephone number, including STD code and, if possible, the extension number of the person you wish to speak with.

Be sure about what subject matter you expect to cover and the result you expect, not forgetting any matter likely to be raised by the person you speak with.

Be sure you have in front of you any information (papers, files, order numbers, etc) relevant to the call.

Choose the time of the call carefully – when the person is likely to be free to accept thc call and, if possible, withln the cheaper rate periods.

Dial carefully, speak clearly, state your name and firm. Develop the conversation naturally in line with your objectives, and listen carefully to the other person's concerns and viewpoint.

Don't prolong the call needlessly, but ensure before you ring off that (a) you know exactly what has been agreed and what action you must take and (b) you have a written record of all key data (eg, name, address and telephone number of caller, account number, quantity and date).

Close the conversation cordially.

Record the key points of the call and ensure appropriate action is taken – including a note to make a repeat call at some future date, if appropriate.

When receiving a call through the operator:

Tell the caller your name (and, if appropriate, department).
Find out what the caller wants.
Respond appropriately.
Ensure that action is jointly agreed, wherever possible.

Don't prolong the call needlessly, but ensure before you ring off that (a) you know exactly what has been agreed and what action you must take and (b) you have a written record of all key data (eg, name, address and telephone number of caller, account number, quantity and date).

Close the conversation cordially.

Record the key points of the call and ensure appropriate action is taken – including a note to make a repeat call at some future date, if appropriate.

When receiving a call directly from outside the firm:

Tell the caller the firm's name, then your name (and, if appropriate, department) and offer to help in a positive and constructive manner.

Find out who the caller should be speaking to, and transfer the call if necessary, keeping the caller informed of any action you take.

If the caller wishes to speak with you, proceed as under receiving a call through the operator.

Formal off-the-job training should be seriously considered for telephone salespeople and for the telephonist. This need not be a long, drawn-out procedure, but the ability to perform consistently and well in the areas outlined in Figures 6 and 10 should be covered. This training should be followed by on-the-job coaching. A couple of days for the off-the-job part should suffice, unless your products, services or conditions of trade are particularly complex.

If your switchboard is not very busy and you have a competent telephone operator, he or she could train the new operator on the job. However, before making this decision, it is important to be sure that the experienced person (a) knows what has to be covered, and (b) is capable of putting this across to the newcomer. The fact that a person is capable of performing a job well does not mean that he or she will be good at teaching someone else to do it.

If you generate income by offering information or advisory services over the telephone, you should consider most carefully the training of the people involved.

ACTION GUIDELINES

1. What are your firm's information-recording and information-processing systems?
2. Which members of your staff ensure that all the key information tasks are properly carried out?
3. Are your staff flexible enough to cover for each other when someone is away? Write down any areas where you could be

at risk if a member of staff became unable to attend work for a while.

4. Do you have any plans to make changes which will involve information flow in the firm? If so, how are you preparing your staff to cope with this?
5. Are all your current office routines really necessary? Has any duplication crept in, or have forms been introduced which are not really needed now?
6. Are you getting good value from your telephones?
7. On the basis of your answers to the above questions, are there some areas where you need to see improvement fast? Attend to these areas as a matter of priority.

CHAPTER 8

Health and Safety

As an entrepreneur, employer or manager, you will need to take steps to ensure, as far as you are able, the health and safety of your employees, your customers and anyone who may visit your premises. In these, as in many other matters, there are legal requirements with which you need to comply. You must also have regard to your neighbours (in terms of noise and other sources of nuisance) and to any material that may leave your premises as refuse, effluent, smoke or vapour.

There are considerations of humanity and business (see Figure 12) in addition to any legal requirements. You must be fully aware of the steps that have to be taken to make safe your premises, the processes you employ and your products and services. Safety depends on an attitude of mind as well as on conditions and prescribed procedures. (The list in Figure 12 is not exhaustive, and does not include, for example, costs arising as a result of claims or legal action by staff, customers or visitors to your premises.)

A high standard of safety-consciousness in a workforce cannot be achieved overnight. It is important to realize that accidents often occur when they are least expected and when there are no obvious reasons. Two of the main causes of accidents are mishandling of goods and falls 'at the same level' (ie, where the ground is level, not inclined or stepped). Accidents occurring during the moving of materials can be minimized by attention to planning and layout, and by training people to lift and shift loads safely. Many falls on level ground could be avoided by good housekeeping, keeping gangways clear and ensuring adequate lighting.

Some hazards are invisible, tasteless and odourless (eg,

X-rays, Microwaves and many gases commonly used or produced in industrial processes), and where these are present, rigorous procedures must be introduced, explained and enforced. There may well be a need to institute a system, for example, which prohibits people from entering certain areas without written authorization from a manager or supervisor who will know for certain that the invisible hazard has been removed (eg, the gas has been dispersed, the X-ray machine isolated from the power supply).

Figure 12 Cost of accidents

Where costs may arise in connection with accidents at the workplace

Minor injuries
Time lost by injured worker
Medical treatment
Time lost by other workers
Damage to machines, tools and materials

More serious injuries
Time lost by injured worker
Medical treatment
Time lost by other workers (sympathy, curiosity, help, lowered morale and possibly lowered productivity)
Injured worker's reduced effectiveness on return to work
Engaging and training a replacement, possibly at lower output
Overtime working to catch up with schedules
Management time in helping, investigating and reporting accident
Loss of production from damaged plant and machinery
Replacement or repair of tools and equipment
Loss of spoilt materials

Anyone who manages an enterprise must ensure that premises, machinery and procedures are safe. Furthermore, each individual has a responsibility to behave in a manner which does not endanger him/herself, or anyone else. It follows that health and safety are part and parcel of the job of all managers and supervisors, and that their training and development must reflect this. This responsibility refers not only to creating safe working conditions and procedures, but also to training people to follow the procedures and ensuring that they adhere to them *in practice.*

It is important to recognize that, although there are some general principles and safety rules, it is imperative that safety is built into the way people are trained to do their daily work and to use the tools, equipment and machinery relevant to their work. For example, workers who use knives and guillotines should be shown how to use them safely; drivers of forklift trucks need to be reminded regularly of the safe way to drive and lift large loads; van drivers who load goods on to their vehicles should be trained how to lift and carry loads safely.

It is important that everyone knows what to do in the case of an accident – for example, how to ensure the emergency services are called, how to operate fire-fighting appliances, how to exit from the building, how to slow down the spread of fire (eg, by closing doors when leaving rooms), where to assemble for roll call. Ideally at least two or three of your people should be trained in first aid, and everyone should know who has received this training. Again there are relevant legal requirements which you must make yourself aware of.

There are, therefore, essentially five steps to safety at work:

- Set up safe workplaces and safe work practices.
- Include general safety rules and procedures, and the reasons for them in every staff member's induction.
- Have initial staff training for carrying out each task in a safe manner.
- Maintain constant vigilance and attention to safety procedures.
- Investigate every accident and take action to prevent any recurrence.

SAFE PLACES AND PRACTICES

This book is not a manual on safety or safety legislation. You must ensure that someone in your firm obtains all the up-to-date information on safe premises, including such elementary considerations as non-slip flooring and floor polish, adequate lighting, and so forth, and also any special precautions due to the nature of the work itself (eg, fume extraction, X-ray screens, visual rest periods for those who use word processors).

Safe practices need to be built into the ordinary daily routine – including fire drills and checks on escape routes – and also included in the way work is arranged and undertaken. Be especially careful about the less obvious dangers – for example, how to lift loads without undue strain, or procedures for handling microbiological or radioactive materials.

The hazards associated with invisible dangers like X-rays (as mentioned above) pose particular problems. People must learn to understand the reason for the precautions. If people are not convinced, for any reason, that the prescribed safety procedures are essential, sooner or later they will ignore them. For example, problems have arisen in the food industry where workers have been known to think that because a batch of foodstuffs is to be autoclaved, the standards of cleanliness can be relaxed, not realizing that the process may not be designed to cope with excessive levels of contamination.

To demand blind adherence to procedures is not enough. Your workforce needs to understand, at least in a basic way, why such procedures are necessary.

SAFETY TRAINING

General safety matters should be covered in the training you give to everybody when they first join the firm (often called 'induction training'). The safety procedures associated with each task to be performed are best included in the training for the task itself, so that it becomes an integral part of the action, and is not regarded as somehow separate.

We all recognize that cutting with a sharp knife or making adjustments to electrical equipment is potentially dangerous, and our training generally incorporates safety procedures. However, it is less easy to remember to teach people to close desk drawers in an office or to ensure that cables from a table lamp or electric typewriter are carefully placed to avoid accidents.

Ideas for topics to be included in safety training are given in Figure 13 (for managers and supervisors) and Figure 14 (for other employees). Elaborate on these topics for your own firm's situation, and make sure these matters are discussed (rather than being the subject of lectures) in relation to your own premises, equipment and procedures. Include as much practical training as possible. You should prepare your own checklist based on the premises, equipment and procedures of your firm. You may also find it useful to look at Figure 15, which deals with safety in the office. *You* must judge how much time and effort to devote to health and safety training, for this will depend, in large part, on how hazardous the activities are in the firm.

Figure 13 Safety training for managers and supervisors

Topics which might be covered in training include:

Responsibility for safe working and accident prevention.
Legal requirements and responsibilities.
General principles of accident prevention.
Causes of accidents and sources of danger.
Fire prevention.
Emergency procedures.
Proper use of safety equipment.
Efficient and safe handling and lifting methods.
Accident investigation and reporting.
Importance of job training using safe practices.
Economics of accident prevention.
Occupational health and safety considerations particular to the operation.
Engineering and maintenance hazards.
Good housekeeping.
Sources of information on safety.

Figure 14 Safety training for other employees

Make sure every employee learns:

How to do each appointed task safely and efficiently.
What hazards exist in any part of the premises where they might enter, and how to deal with these.
Why each safety procedure is necessary.
Their personal responsibility for avoiding accidents to themselves and others.

Emergency procedures, including fire drills.
Proper use of safety equipment provided.
The importance of good housekeeping in the prevention of accidents.
Location of first-aid box and names of first-aiders.

Figure 15 Office safety

Offices seem to be safe places – they are not. To emphasize this, the following topics might be covered in a safety course for office workers.

Beware of:
Worn or missing stair treads.
Missing or damaged handrails.
Worn floor coverings.
Slippery floor surfaces.
Broken glass, etc.
Trailing telephone or electric leads.

Don't cause accidents through furniture by:
Leaving desk drawers open.
Opening more than one filing cabinet drawer at a time (filing alphabetically from the bottom drawer upwards reduces the likelihood of tilting the cabinet).
Putting furniture where sharp corners protrude.
Standing on swivel chairs.
Leaving obstructions such as furniture, cartons and trolleys in gangways or passages.

Avoid fires by:
Using ashtrays for cigarettes, not the waste bin.
Disposing of waste paper and other flammable material regularly and frequently.
Switching off machines at night and removing the plugs.
Being careful where you stand portable heaters.
Not placing paper, towels or clothing over portable heaters.

Prepare for fires by:
Learning the fire instructions.
Learning how to use fire-fighting equipment.

Learning the exit routes and assembly points.
Learning how to behave in case of fire.
Learning escape routes which avoid lifts.

Use electrical equipment carefully. Report:
Loose connections.
Unearthed equipment.
Damaged cables.
Defective insulation.
Overloaded circuits.
Broken switches.
Appliances in a dangerous state.
Trailing leads.

Use machinery properly by:
Reading instructions carefully.
Ensuring safety guards are in place.
Stopping machinery before cleaning.
Learning how to stop machinery in emergency.
Keeping your fingers clear of blades (eg, of a guillotine).

Lift and carry carefully:
Keep your back straight and use your leg muscles to lift.
Share heavy loads with someone else.
Be sure you can see over the top of a load.
Don't carry at one time more than you can safely and comfortably manage.

List is adapted from Is My Office Safe? HMSO.

SAFETY AS A WAY OF LIFE

Approach the gates of a firm which deals in dangerous and flammable materials and you will be confronted with large notices warning you to extinguish cigarettes and to hand in at the gatehouse any matches, lighters or electrical gadgets which could cause a spark or produce heat. Walk about the plant and you will see more notices at strategic places, reminding you of the hazards. Talk to any of the people about their work or training and the question of safety and safe working practices will come up in the conversation over and over again.

In such places safety has, rightly, become a regular topic of concern and conversation. It has become part of the culture – 'the way we do things around here'. Anyone who does not display the same concern with safety sticks out like a sore thumb. They are not welcome. They must conform or depart. This may sound harsh, but hundreds or even many thousands of lives could be at stake, as well as vast sums of money.

It is almost impossible for the ordinary firm, where such hazards are not evident, to emulate this somewhat extreme example. Nevertheless, good managers can create a 'culture' where people who do their work safely and considerately are regarded as members of the team, and the maverick who behaves carelessly is frowned upon.

The case of the forklift truck driver is an interesting one from this point of view. It is not difficult for such drivers to feel like 'cowboys', skilfully steering their steeds through the gangways and picking up large loads with casual abandon. The 'culture' should consider such persons a menace, and regard highly drivers who take care to load their trucks evenly, who drive their vehicle in the knowledge that someone could walk into their path, and who realize how dangerous and costly it can be to bump into a pile of goods.

Gaining and maintaining such a safety-conscious culture is not a once-for-all matter – it requires constant attention. The example of the senior people comes first. Then there is the induction or initial training of other staff. This should be followed up, as appropriate, by brightly-painted posters which draw attention to particular hazards. Such posters, however, soon become part of the background: they must be changed from time to time or they will lose their effect.

If you have regular meetings with senior people, make sure that safety comes up regularly. One way to spark off such a discussion is to ask a person to look around the premises with particular regard to health and safety matters (eg, for fire doors wedged open, guards not secured, slippery floors, materials blocking gangways or staircases, broken bulbs not replaced, etc). Safety audits cascade through management structure and, if used correctly (ie, with praise and displeasure where appropriate), have a place in motivating people to improve and maintain the standards necessary. What gets measured gets done. Any accidents – even where no injuries occur – should be discussed at such meetings, not just to try to prevent recurrence, but also because this helps to keep safety at the forefront of people's minds.

It is a good idea to consult all the people who work for you about safety matters, either directly or, if you have a large staff, through representatives. In larger firms, there should be safety representatives and a safety committee where health and safety matters can be kept under review.

Some firms have experimented with competitions for the safest department, office, etc – with considerable success. Such competitions are best conducted over several months so that sound habits are formed. Make sure you involve people in setting the standards, and ensure that the arrangements and judging are seen to be fair by all concerned.

INVESTIGATING ACCIDENTS

If you are unfortunate enough to have an accident at the workplace, you must comply with the statutory requirements on reporting it. At the same time, the way the incident is investigated can be a valuable learning experience for those concerned. If you want to get the most learning out of the situation, don't focus your attention on who was responsible, but try to decide how it happened, what procedure was being followed that might be modified, what equipment was being used that might be guarded or adjusted in some way.

If the correct procedure was not being followed, don't shrug the accident off as carelessness by staff. See if there is some aspect of the procedure which is unduly irksome. If so, the likelihood is that someone else, sooner or later, will deviate from the prescribed method and cause another accident. Be prepared to see if the procedure can be changed to be less irksome, but equally safe.

If the people involved became inattentive, ask yourself if the procedure can be modified so that those involved are motivated to pay attention and stay alert. Drivers who report feeling drowsy on a boring dead-straight motorway often find that a motorway with gentle curves, which present changing scenery ahead, is less soporific. The same can be true of routine work in a factory, where inattention can lead to equally disastrous results.

Many large companies display accident statistics, and a particularly useful figure to display is the number of days without an accident at the site, as this encourages people to maintain the record and it is generally more beneficial to quote a number that becomes higher with success.

SAFETY AUDITS

It must be obvious from what has been said that the management of safety involves being constantly on the look-out for hazards and being prepared to take swift action to deal with them, whether they are due to sloppy housekeeping (material left in gangways, drawers of filing cabints left open, oil spilled on the floor) or to defective equipment, fixtures or fittings.

In some companies, senior managers, often accompanied by safety officers, formally inspect premises from time to time, including storage as well as work areas, and make notes against a checklist of items which indicate whether the housekeeping and standard of maintenance is adequate. Marks can be awarded against the items, thereby encouraging the positive management of safety.

ACTION GUIDELINES

1. Who is responsible for ensuring that your workplaces and methods are safe? Does that individual have the competence, authority and time to do this job properly, bearing in mind that he or she may need access to expert help and advice?
2. Are you satisfied that the induction training given to each and every newcomer to the workforce adequately covers all the health and safety aspects involved in your firm – including the safety of visitors and customers?
3. Are you satisfied that the initial task-training given to your employees pays due consideration to safety matters and areas of potential risk?
4. Have you created a positive and conscious attitude towards health and safety so that people regard it as sensible and right to maintain constant vigilance in these matters?
5. Do you have a sound procedure for investigating any accident or potentially dangerous incident such that people look for positive ways to prevent a recurrence?
6. Have you ensured that you comply with all relevant legislation and other standards, codes of practice and authoritative guidance in this field, and that you have a

means of keeping up-to-date on any changes which might affect your business?

7. Have you considered whether it would be useful, in your particular company, to display accident statistics or to conduct periodic safety audits?

CHAPTER 9

DEVELOPING THE POTENTIAL OF SPECIALISTS

Many firms – including smaller businesses – now use sophisticated scientific methods of manufacture and control, where there is a need to match technological prowess with sound business sense. The engineer-scientist, technologist or computer specialist tends to look at the world differently from the way a businessperson does. Often the training such specialists receive at university does not prepare them adequately for the harsh world of commerce where costs have to be contained while quality is preserved.

Maintaining the technological edge while remaining financially sound means that a way must be found for ensuring that engineers and technologists who work for you understand the principles of business and, in particular, the essential features of management accounting. A second area where specialists may have something to learn is that of dealing with other people – non-specialists – who work in the firm. You may well find a third area where they need to do some learning: that is, in the particular way in which their subject is used in your firm.

It is important to recognize that in any scientific, engineering or technological discipline the amount of knowledge is now vast, so that a university or college course can do no more than give the basic grounding in the language and concepts involved. If you operate at the frontier of knowledge, then the likelihood is that the specialist has a lot of reading to do to get, and remain, on top of the subject as it applies in your firm. It has been said that the amount of knowledge in a given subject area can easily double in just ten years.

In terms of their specialist knowledge, it is important to recruit people who are appropriate to your firm. Once you have recruited the experts, there are three particular areas where you need to be sure that they are competent, and where help with training and development may be called for:

1. The firm and its business
2. Dealing with people
3. In-depth specialist knowledge and skills.

The introduction of new technological devices often brings other changes in its wake, and managing the overall process of change is a skill which few engineers, scientists, technologists or computer specialists acquire during their education. You may need to take steps to ensure that those involved in making changes get the training and support they need to cope with such problems and challenges. This is explored more fully in the next chapter. If change is to be brought about with minimum disruption and maximum benefit, it is essential to inform people at an early stage, and to involve them in discussions and decisions which will affect their work.

ROLE OF SPECIALISTS

How are specialists used? Your specialists may be engaged in fundamental research as the basis of future developments or, more probably, on development work to prepare new products and services for trials in the market-place. In some firms, specialists work closely with customers to develop products which meet their specific needs.

Some scientists and technologists are employed on quality control work, testing the products at various stages to ensure that they are satisfactory. Computer specialists may be involved in systems analysis and programming, (a) to improve the firm's efficiency, (b) as a service to customers, or (c) to design products and services for the market-place. The extent to which specialists need knowledge of the business clearly depends on their roles, but in every case some familiarization is required.

Every specialist will have to be able to work reasonably harmoniously with other people in the firm, and some will need to engage with your customers. It is not good enough to throw specialists in at the deep end. You must take steps to ensure that they can get along with people and, in particular, that they know how to listen and to interpret the problems of customers.

THE FIRM'S BUSINESS

What aspects of the business should each specialist in your firm know about? Only you and your senior colleagues can answer that question, but you may get some clues from the checklist provided in Figure 16. Go through the items one by one, and add any that you think are missing.

Every reasonably senior member of your staff should know the aims and objectives of the firm. Are you aiming at a particular turnover or market share? Are you at an expansion phase, or set to consolidate your existing levels of production or service, improving quality and ensuring a sound base for later growth?

Anyone involved in research or development would wish to know this, and also what business you consider the firm is in. If your firm is making small calculators and hand-held computers, is it in the computer business, or in the leisure business? Should you be looking for improvements in the products and software to convert them into companions for the travelling businessperson or tools for the sixth-form student, or into sophisticated toys for next Christmas's bright young 12-year-olds?

The durability, price and appearance of your products depend on such factors as much as on the materials available for construction and on the power of the component hardware and software available. These are, therefore, fundamental inputs to the design – along with an idea of what price tag your intended customers will tolerate. Don't forget who has the disposable income if you want to operate in a particular area of the leisure trade.

Figure 16 Knowledge of the business

The following items are some of the areas where your specialists may need knowledge of the business. Look through the list and tick off items where you consider that knowledge and skills would enable the specialist to do his or her job more effectively. Remember that the particular role of the specialist will have a bearing on what knowledge is important.

- The aims and objectives of the firm.
- The essential business of the firm.

- The basic structure of the firm; who does what.
- The products or services provided by the firm.
- The customers served by the firm.
- The firm's marketing strategy.
- The key quality features of the firm's output.
- The business environment for the firm.
- The technology and work processes employed.
- The key areas where costs are incurred.
- The main sources of profit.

If your firm makes central heating boilers, are you simply in the business of providing these boilers, or are you part and parcel of the central heating industry, including the extensive DIY trade? If you are in central heating, you must consider modern methods of temperature control, and the extent to which people will opt for air conditioning as well as space heating. How well does your product line up with this?

Is the boiler readily adapted for use with computer-controlled systems? If it simple enough for the DIY enthusiast to fit and bring into service? Can the ordinary householder fit lagging around it? Considerations of this sort should inform the people developing products for next year's markets – or for later this year. Should you be developing a range of products to accompany your basic unit? Should there be simple booklets showing how it should be fitted, lagged and maintained?

These two illustrations demonstrate that the specialists concerned with development work should be working hand-in-glove with the marketing and sales people, and in tune with your strategy.

Analogous considerations apply to specialists concerned with setting and maintaining quality standards (eg, for engineered products or for chemicals). They should understand clearly the trade-offs between quality and price, and the relationship between quality and customer satisfaction in the particular market you operate. Not every customer wants the highest quality irrespective of the price. The quality demanded is thus a function of safety, utility and price. Who will use the products, what for and under what circumstances?

Take as an example a firm manufacturing canned stew. If it is making this to be sold over the counter in shops, the quality of the stew must be good in the customer's judgment; comply with relevant food legislation; and be attractively presented, often with brightly printed paper labels. If, however, the food is intended as army rations in the Tropics, different criteria apply. The stew must still be acceptable in quality, and conform to any relevant regulations and standards laid down. But there is no need for a paper label – indeed, this might be a nuisance, as the label or gum may accelerate the deterioration of the can in damp tropical conditions. Facts about the customer and applications are essential to a sound quality assurance function.

DEALING WITH PEOPLE

We saw earlier that specialists will have to be able to collaborate with other people in the firm (indeed, in a small firm virtually everyone must be willing and able to work with other people). If, before joining your firm, the specialists have been working in an ordinary industrial or commercial concern, the likelihood is that they will have learned how to work constructively with people of different backgrounds and interests – although it is as well to check this out. Those who have come from a university or research establishment may still have some rough edges in social skill terms.

They may be used to the cut and thrust of scientific debate with colleagues; talking jargon to other people who understand it; and working with people who are motivated to make discoveries and understand what makes things tick. Now they find themselves with people who don't care about how the machine or product works, but whether it will do the job. Specialists in the business world are surrounded by people who don't know the jargon – and don't want to know it.

They may have come from a background where they did not have to account for every penny spent, but now all expenditure comes out of the firm's profits. Scientists are trained to design experiments which eliminate human feelings and prejudices – the very stuff of which ordinary interactions between people are made. It is not surprising that specialists who come from such a background may need help in adjusting and learning to work effectively with the people in your organization. In most cases the problems are not as acute as this, but this is the kind of pressure in the background. (Fortunately, many specialists have had 'humanizing' experiences in social clubs and the like.)

Those who do find it difficult to handle their relationships with people at the workplace will require help in developing social skills, especially listening, as explained in Chapter 18.

IN-DEPTH KNOWLEDGE

If your firm employs specialized equipment which has been bought in, it may be worth making arrangements for your new specialists to visit the manufacturer, and perhaps to take a course with them. Thus they may be able to learn at first hand the underlying theory of the equipment, how it is intended to be used and its full capabilities. All too often, firms that purchase expensive equipment fail to use it to its full potential, so that a less sophisticated – and less costly – piece of equipment would have sufficed. If you pay a lot of money for equipment, make sure you have people who can use it to the full extent, so that it is of real value to the enterprise.

If you are using unusual materials, the specialists can probably learn all they need to know from the relevant literature – the manufacturer's publications, textbooks, reference books and journals.

If your firm has developed specialist materials or equipment, then newcomers must learn about these from you and your existing staff. They must learn about the properties, characteristics and potential of your wares from relevant written company material, diagrams, etc, and above all from coaching provided by key people in your organization. Remember that specialists should be accustomed to absorbing information from written material, tables, diagrams, and the like, but coaching makes the data come alive and assists in the understanding of complex ideas and principles.

ACTION GUIDELINES

1. Be careful to recruit specialists who will fit into your firm, in terms of their expertise and personal qualities.
2. Be clear about the role of each specialist you employ, and ensure that he or she has the requisite skills – business and interpersonal as well as technical – needed to succeed in the job.
3. Where necessary, take steps to ensure that specialists

understand the rudiments of the business, and where the profit comes from.

4. Where necessary, assist specialists to develop interpersonal skills, especially in communicating with non-specialists, both inside and outside the firm.
5. Recognize that even specialists may need to spend time learning about the specific applications of their knowledge to your products and services: assist them.
6. Recognize that specialists need to keep up to date, especially in areas where technological growth is fast.

CHAPTER 10

LEARNING TO MANAGE CHANGE

The need for change in your firm may arise out of the needs of the market-place or from your desire to improve the effectiveness of your operation. The products and services you provide may need to change as your customers' demands alter. In a healthy firm change will be normal: the time to get really worried is if everything seems to stay the same.

Increases in the price of the raw materials or fuel you use, or in the cost of storage space, may lead to a reappraisal of the way the work is organized. New developments in technology or materials may come along which can be used to improve efficiency in your manufacturing process; in the services you offer; or in the way you handle information and manage paperwork. As the firm grows to meet demand, more space or faster and more sophisticated machines may be needed.

The introduction of new machinery or procedures is all too often followed by a series of frustrating and sometimes costly incidents. Contrary to expectation, new methods often fail to give the return on investment as quickly as planned. We frequently excuse all this as 'teething troubles', as if such unplanned stoppages are just natural and to be expected. In reality, many of these pitfalls can be foreseen and avoided if the proper preparations are made for the introduction of changes (ie, if the changes are managed).

How can you set about managing the next change you wish to introduce? There are three particular aspects which must be covered. There is a need to set out the key steps in the process, taking into account the human aspects of the problem as well as the normal critical path analysis factors. Before you can do this, however, you need to make sure you have thought through how you will cope with the two key factors as far as your people are concerned: their attitudes to the proposed changes, and their ability to handle the installation and operation of the new machinery and/or methods envisaged.

In this chapter, we will not discuss what action to take when you know that people will be made redundant because of new technology, or when you know that people's jobs will become boring. These are very real problems, and they are discussed in Chapter 20. In general, the more notice people have about changes which affect them, the more ready they are to consider them coolly and logically, and to seek ways to cope.

ATTITUDES TO CHANGE

First of all, let's be clear about one thing: everybody is to some extent apprehensive about change until they understand it and feel that they will be able to cope with it. If you announce suddenly that a new machine is to be introduced into the firm or that some new procedure must be adopted, don't be surprised if people are apprehensive or even a little hostile. That is a perfectly natural reaction; and it is one of the key factors that you, as a manager, must take into account in the way you handle change.

If you wish to minimize this reluctance or hostility to change, there are some simple actions you can take. Bear in mind that these adverse attitudes arise basically from fear of the unknown; and are heightened by sudden announcements of imminent change, or a feeling of being pressurized into situations where unforeseen difficulties can arise.

People feel threatened when they are not sure they are going to cope and succeed in a new situation, or when they think they are being pushed into things without having the time to understand why. The possible natural responses to fear are threefold: fighting, flight or coping. In modern society, the fighting or flight may not mean actually lashing out or running away, but rather reactions such as refusing to recognize and respond to reality, or putting obstacles in the way of progress. Part of the manager's job is to help people to learn how to deal with these fears and to cope with change.

Fear of the unknown can be dealt with in only one way: people must learn about the new machines and/or methods. Shock, which is accentuated by suddenness, can be reduced by giving people adequate notice. If you announce unexpectedly on Friday evening, to a group of people who are unfamiliar with the machines, that all the manual typewriters will be replaced by word processors next Monday, or that your lathes will be replaced by numerically-controlled machines, or that new tills will be installed in your shop over the weekend, don't be surprised if your staff become unhappy and even hostile.

Giving people notice of proposals and innovations is not just common courtesy or good human relations; it is actually an effective way to manage if you want to enhance people's capacity to change.

How do you deal with the feeling of pressure? People feel pressurized when they can't really see the point of what they are being asked to do, and when it makes fresh demands on them without seeming to offer any advantages. Helping them understand the new methods and procedures is an advantage, but it doesn't go far enough. What they really need, if they are to fall in with your plans whole-heartedly, is to understand why the new machines and/or methods are being introduced.

If it is feasible, and often it will be in a smaller firm or department, the best way to help people understand the need for change is to involve them in discussions about the proposals as early as possible, perhaps even before the final decision is made. Presumably the proposed changes arise because you have specific aims in mind, and you have thought through carefully how these can be achieved. Often in conversation with your people, they may put forward a better solution to the problem, or help you see how to achieve your aims in a better way. Even if your own original ideas are still the best, talking it through with your people will enable them to understand why change is needed; and they are then more likely to want to help you make a success of it.

In larger firms, it is not prudent to discuss major changes with everybody at the same time. You will need to think through, carefully, step by step, who should be told, and what they should be told, spreading out the information and consultation process downwards from the top, and outwards to each section which is involved. It is still wise to ensure that everyone has had an opportunity to comment and to appreciate what the change will mean before it actually happens.

In larger firms, you may need to consult representatives of your employees, but in such cases it is wise to ensure that you communicate directly with every member of staff, preferably in writing and at a meeting or series of meetings.

What can you do about the fear of not being able to work the new equipment or follow the new procedures? Adults don't like to look foolish among their workmates. Supervisors don't want to be ignorant of the new machinery which is being brought into the firm. The answer to this question may well be orthodox training. Send them on a course to learn what they need to know, and to acquire any special skills, or make arrangements for them to be properly taught on your own premises. Many equipment manufacturers offer courses for the staff of firms who purchase their wares. (Be careful, however, because although generally such courses cover the elementary operation of the equipment well, further training may be needed for your particular firm to exploit the full potential of your purchase.)

This may not always be enough. At an even earlier stage, it may help if the people concerned can visit another firm where the equipment is in use. Just seeing and talking with ordinary people using the equipment on an everyday basis may be enough to dispel fears of this kind. Your people will come back saying, 'Well, if you can learn to do it, I'm sure I can too'. Coping with change is, for the people concerned, an individual problem as well as a problem for the group and the organization. Each person must cope with it in his or her own way and context. The help you give should take this perspective into account.

Many firms are introducing new computer systems and word processors. For an older person who has never used, or even seen, one before, being confronted with such equipment can be a daunting experience. (Most young people, who may not suffer from the mature person's inhibitions, seem to take to them quickly.) Why not tuck the computer terminal away in a little room, or in a quiet corner, and encourage your people to spend, say, half an hour from time to time working on a very simple programme? Once the mystery has gone, the way is open for serious training.

All this may seem an awful waste of time. But it is an investment in your people, in their understanding, in their abilities and in their goodwill. The pay-off comes when you try to make the changes work. What's the point of investing a lot of money in new equipment if you are not prepared to invest some time in the people who will work it? Refer to the summary in Figure 17 (on page 86).

Many changes will involve people working together in new ways, and you may need to consider how to encourage teamworking and closer understanding and collaboration between people.

Figure 17 Change and learning needs

Write down precisely what changes you propose to introduce.

Who will be most directly affected?

What new knowledge and skills will they require:
a) to operate the new machine or procedure?
b) to cope with any related changes (eg, time to do other tasks)?
c) to manage any new work relationships (eg, with people whose work will now impinge on the person concerned)?

Apart from the people most closely affected by the new procedures, what other people will have different responsibilities or work patterns as a result of the changes? Include:
a) the manager of the people concerned
b) anyone whose work is related to that of the people concerned, eg, storekeeper, maintenance engineer, operator who provides materials to be used on new machine, person who purchases spare parts or consumable materials concerned with machine operation.

In each case write down what new knowledge and skills they will require.

In thinking about people who require competence to manage change, do not forget to include the people who choose the new equipment, or design the new procedures. What learning have they done to equip them for this task?

(In the case of choosing equipment, for example, the learning may have to be achieved by visiting exhibitions, reading appropriate technical magazines and talking with other people with similar problems, before contacting equipment manufacturers. There is a need to learn which questions to ask.)

ABILITIES

One of the reasons for 'teething troubles' is that managers don't always think through who will be affected by the introduction of new equipment or procedures. They may train the individual concerned to operate the new machine: the craftsman, or the typist. But what of the consequential changes – in work patterns, work flows and working relationships? Have these been thought through? Who else will be concerned? If the new machine is more readily adjusted to making different products, or if the throughput is much faster than before, what is the effect on the supply of materials to the machine, and what arrangements have to be made to remove and store the finished goods?

If the speed of the machine means that the individual concerned can get through this work in half the time, how will the rest of the person's time be spent? Does the person concerned need training to undertake other tasks? If the machine is expensive, you may want to reduce down-time to a minimum. This could mean making sure that you have enough people trained to use it, so that when holidays or sickness arise your machine can still go on producing. Another step you may wish to take to reduce down-time is to ensure that someone in your outfit can handle straightforward breakdowns, so that the servicing engineer is called in only rarely.

If you decide to introduce audio typing, don't forget that the managers who will do the dictating need training just as much as the people who will do the typing. Furthermore, if there are particular hazards attached to the operation of the new machinery or procedures, everyone involved should be trained to cope with these. (Refer to the Action Guidelines at the end of this chapter to aid you in deciding the learning needs of yourself and your people.)

KEY STEPS

It is worthwhile drawing up your own simple critical path for this whole exercise, taking into account the 'people issues' discussed above, as well as the usual factors. The elements you will need to build into your plan are:

- The purpose of the changes proposed.
- Discussion of the matter, as far as possible, with the people who will be most affected by the changes.

- Consideration, with the key people, of alternative ways of achieving the desired improvements.
- A critical path analysis for the introduction of the new equipment/procedures.
- Implementation of the plan, including placing orders for new equipment/materials; designing new procedures/forms, etc; testing new documentation; preparing services for equipment.
- Familiarization of key staff with the basics of the equipment/procedures.
- Training, as appropriate, for the staff involved.
- Full briefing of technical staff responsible for installation.
- Adequate warning of delivery dates, etc to key staff.
- Proper supervision of installation and maintenance.
- On-the-job training and coaching to ensure efficient commissioning of new equipment and procedures.
- After a period, a review of the effectiveness of the new methods, involving all the key staff.

Most of this is straightforward, but it is amazing how often some key step is left out in practice. One of the commonest problems is a failure to take into account everyone who will be affected by the change. Will a new machine, for example, do the work much more quickly and thus influence the storage space requirements? Will it increase the documentation required? Will it require special maintenance tools or lubricants? Careful thought at the outset about the ramifications of new equipment and procedures could save a lot of time and trouble (and hence cash) later on when you are trying to get machines going at full stretch.

In learning about choosing equipment, much may be achieved by visiting exhibitions, reading appropriate technical magazines and talking with other people with similar problems, before contacting equipment manufacturers. (There is a need to learn which questions to ask.)

ACTION GUIDELINES

1. Write down precisely what changes you propose to introduce.
2. Write down the names and job titles of the people most directly affected.
3. Identify the new knowledge and skills they will require:
   - to operate the new machine or procedure
   - to cope with any related changes (eg, time to do other tasks)
   - to manage any new work relationships (eg, with people whose work will now impinge on the person concerned).
4. Apart from the people most closely affected by the new procedures, identify other people who will have different responsibilities or work patterns as a result of the changes. Include:
   - the manager of the people concerned
   - anyone whose work is related to that of the people concerned (eg, storekeeper; maintenance engineer, operator who provides materials to be used on new machine; person who purchases spare parts or consumable materials concerned with machine operation).
5. In each case write down what new knowledge and skills they will require.
6. In thinking about people who require competence to manage change, don't forget to include the people who choose the new equipment, or design the new procedures. What learning have they done to equip them for this task?

CHAPTER 11

LEARNING TO MANAGE TIME

Talk to anyone who tries to run a business – large or small – and almost invariably they will tell you that they do not have enough time to do everything properly. As well as trying to provide goods and services, there are many administrative and financial matters that require attention, and it seems that there are never enough hours in the day. In these circumstances it is all too easy to attend to urgent problems and to neglect the important matters on which your long-term prosperity depends.

How do you and your top people get time to think and plan ahead? The likelihood is that you are finding it difficult to get enough time to read this book! But read on, for help is at hand. Working through this chapter is an investment. Do the job properly and the time you will save on a day-to-day basis will pay for this book – and for the time you have taken to read through it. To gain this bonus, however, you really must *work through* this chapter. Simply reading it will not do.

You can work through it on your own, or you might try working through it with some senior people in your firm. Working through this material with your top team means that you should be ready to help each other to make more profitable use of your time.

VALUE OF TIME

First do a rough calculation. What is the cost, to the firm, of 15 minutes of your time? Get a rough estimate by writing down your annual salary and dividing it by 5,000. That means that if your gross annual salary is £40,000, every 15 minutes you waste costs the firm £8, and every hour £32. (If you want a better estimate, use Figure 18 as a starting point.) The more important figure, and one that is more difficult to estimate, is what you may have cost the firm in terms of lost orders or ill-considered decisions as you rush to make up the wasted time.

Figure 18 Annual cost of manager time

Gross salary.
Firm's contribution to national insurance.
Firm's contribution to pension.
Motoring, travel and subsistence costs.
Office accommodation costs (calculate rent, rates, heating, lighting, telephone, depreciation of desk, chairs, cabinets, etc).
Secretarial assistance and pension contributions, provision of space, heating, lighting, telephone, depreciation of desk, chair, typewriter, etc).
Sundries – newspapers, periodicals, etc.
Any other costs connected with the employment of a manager.

Note

Roughly, a senior executive costs a firm twice as much as his or her salary, and works for about 40 hours a week for, say, 230 days per year (allowing five weeks' holiday). In smaller firms, the boss generally works for more than 50 hours a week, sometimes a good deal longer, for 240 days a year.

Calculate the cost of a two-hour meeting involving yourself and four of your senior people. A rough estimate will do. Staggering, isn't it? Be sure that next time you get value for money from that kind of meeting.

By getting senior staff to work out these figures for themselves, you can discuss them and begin to instil a sense of the value of executive time. Don't give people figures you have calculated yourself: this reduces the impact of the figures and decreases the learning which takes place.

If you want to improve your use of time, there are basically two problems you must tackle. First, find out how time is spent (an apt word). Second, establish what your personal objectives are and see that your time is purposefully used to achieve these objectives (ie, how time can be used profitably).

These two issues should be of concern to anyone in your firm who has to organize his or her time (ie, the people who are not tied down by the routine of tending a machine or following clerical procedures). The more people there are who are responsible for scheduling their own work, and the higher paid they are, the greater is your firm's need for good time management.

SPENDING TIME

You are all so busy. Where does this time go? The chances are that you really don't know. The best way to find out is to keep a simple diary for a typical week. Don't choose a week when two or three of your senior people are away, so that their work is combined with your own. Don't choose a week that is easy because everything is quiet. There's no such thing as an average week for most managers and certainly not for the boss of a small firm, but try to choose a reasonably typical period that's coming along soon.

Get your secretary to make up a set of 'time use sheets', similar to the pattern in Figure 19, but to suit your own lifestyle and purpose. Fill in a new sheet for each day of the week. Begin by writing down the three or four main things you want to do that day. Be specific, not woolly. Express these items in terms of what you hope to achieve (eg, 'Agree production targets for next month with production manager' or 'Decide on which vehicles to purchase to replace existing vans after discussion with distribution manager', rather than 'See production manager about targets' or 'Discuss replacement vehicles with distribution manager').

Keep your 'time use sheet' on your desk or by your side wherever you are. Complete the first three columns (time, activity and duration) as the day proceeds. Be sure to include every telephone call and every other interruption. Fill it up promptly, at least once an hour. It is no good leaving it until lunchtime or the end of the day, for you will forget the very detail you need. If you find you have missed out a chunk of time, do your best to remember what you did, what happened, and how long each item lasted.

Make sure each entry is as explicit as possible. For example, 'Review stock levels with JK' rather than 'Discussion with JK'.

Use abbreviations which you will recognize later to save writing time. Include travelling time in your record, and, if you read business papers on the train, make a note of this.

This is all a chore, but you will not have to do it often and the exercise should prove most enlightening. If you can't do it, where is your self-discipline? Do you need a course in self-management as well?

Make sure you make a new entry at least every 15 minutes, even if it is only 'Ditto'. You may think the time interval of 15 minutes is too short, but it is a fact of life that most managers

Figure 19 Time-use sheet

Day: Date:

The four main things I want to achieve today are:

1. Progress:

2. Progress:

3. Progress:

4. Progress:

Time	Activity	Duration	Notes

Total time spent:

spend much of their time working on things for only a few minutes before another demand comes along. Uninterrupted thought is a luxury for most managers during working hours in small firms. If you set aside time out of normal working hours (eg, in the evening or at weekends) for business purposes, make a note of this as well.

At the end of each day during the period, turn to the objectives listed at the top of your 'time-use sheet' and make a note opposite 'progress' on how far you consider you moved towards your goal. Next, look through the items listed on your 'time-use sheet' and make a note alongside on the value of the activity. Was this time well spent? Should this matter have been dealt with by someone else? Did it take a lot longer than necessary? Had you prepared adequately for the discussion?

You may well start to find areas where you need to improve performance even at this stage. Make a special note of how long you spend in uninterrupted activity, free of visitors and telephone calls. See if you can estimate, from your 'time-use sheet', the average time you spend free from interruptions.

Look through your 'time-use sheet' and identify where you have not used time profitably. Managers typically use up time in a number of ways, as listed in Figure 20. Look carefully through this list, and in the light of your 'time-use sheet' records tick off any areas where you would like to see a definite improvement in your own use of time.

Figure 20 Time-use improvement

Seeking information Would you spend less time at this if your sources of information were better organized?

Reading material Are you sure you have selected the right material to read, and have you developed an effective way of sifting through the text to find and retain the important facts and ideas?

Managing conversations Would your conversations with people, in person or on the telephone, be more effective if you thought more about what you were hoping to achieve, and how to structure the conversation to improve the chances of success?

Managing interruptions Would your time be better spent if you asked some people to telephone or come back another time, or to take their problems to someone else, or to be more precise in what they are requesting?

Attending meetings Are there ways in which you can structure meetings to make them more effective?

Containing socializing Some social interaction is helpful in 'greasing the wheels' when people work together, but are there occasions when this gets out of hand and wastes time?

Undelegated responsbilities Are you still accepting queries and making decisions in areas which you should have delegated, so that your time is wasted while the person who should be responsible is confused and frustrated?

Adjusting objectives Are you changing your mind about objectives in response to changes in the situation, or because you have not taken the trouble to think them through properly in the first place?

Clarifying responsibilities Although this is necessary from time to time, are you doing this very often because people in your firm are generally not sure who is supposed to be responsible for what?

Opening communications Are you often dealing with failures in communication between people in the firm (ie, treating the symptom rather than the disease of poor communication)?

Deferring action Are you confident that each time you defer a decision or action there are sound reasons for doing so, or is this indecision merely wasting time?

Estimating time Have you developed the skill of estimating reasonably accurately how long tasks take, or are you constantly put out when tasks take longer than the time you had allowed?

Containing crises Have you a strategy for coping with unexpected crises in a way that does not unduly disrupt progress towards the achievement of your objectives, or do such occurrences throw your plans off balance for days?

Self-management Have you developed an effective personal strategy for managing your time and your paperwork, or are you constantly dashing from one crisis to another?

USING TIME

Figure 20 is a list of ways in which managers typically waste time. In most cases spending *some* time on such matters is justifiable and useful, but all too often more time is spent than is required. Go through the list and tick off any item where you consider improvements can be made in your firm. Choose priorities and work on these along the lines described below.

INFORMATION

This is crucial in any manager's life and it comes from several sources. Over a period of time you should be able to recognize the kind of information you really need – about your firm's activities (output, sales, key cost figures, etc); about the market-place; about your competitors; about relevant technology; about shipping movements, and so forth. Then you must set up the simple systems to provide you with that information from time to time, and ensure you have quick access to relevant reference books and periodicals.

The selection of appropriate reading matter is essential. Choose matter which gives you the information you need to run your firm successfully. If you want to read a particular magazine because it interests you, OK, but don't call it work unless it is really relevant. You may be bombarded with advertising literature, and you must develop the ability to assess its relevance quickly and consign all unwanted material to the waste-paper bin, pronto.

CONVERSATIONS AND MEETINGS

A major part of the time of most managers is spent in conversations, face-to-face or on the telephone. Much of this is necessary and productive. However, a good deal of time is also wasted in this way because people do not think clearly about what they want out of the conversation, or make sure at the outset that they check out the other person's expectations. (See Figure 11 on page 60 for some hints on using the telephone to good effect.) In practice many of the same issues arise in respect of face-to-face conversations – especially the one about making sure each person knows what has been agreed before they part company. (Have a look at Chapter 18 too.)

How often have you come away from a meeting and said to a colleague, 'That was a waste of time'? Remember how much meetings cost? You can't afford to waste them. Be sure that you have a clear aim for the meeting; that the right people attend; that the objectives are made clear; and that the time is spent pursuing these objectives in the most effective manner.

If you deal with people, you do need to spend some time socializing, enquiring after their health, and the like. This is particularly important when you are meeting people for the first time or people you do not meet often. Without it, it takes longer to establish a rapport and to move to an effective conversation. However, socializing can get out of hand and cause time to be wasted. The only solution is for people to become more aware of the problem; as soon as you realize this is happening, find an inoffensive way of moving on to the business in hand.

DELEGATION

As firms grow, it becomes necessary for the top person to delegate increasing amounts of responsibility to other people. It is natural to want to keep in touch with all that is happening and to know about all the decisions being made, but it simply isn't possible. The top manager must disengage from many of the day-to-day decisions and let other people get on with it. How do you do this? It is not as easy as it sounds.

You will be happy to delegate only when you have confidence in the people who work for you. The way to build up this confidence is to:

- choose people you can trust
- ensure that they have the knowledge and skills to do the job, using training and coaching
- trust them with small decisions, and as they prove themselves, increase the level of responsibility.

Allocating responsibility to others on this basis gives the manager more time to look ahead and plan for the future. It gives the individual a sense of being respected and valued, and helps to motivate him or her to give their best. It also helps the individual to feel more involved and loyal.

DEFINING OBJECTIVES AND RESPONSIBILITIES

Some managers seem to be always changing their mind about what really matters, about what their objectives are. Naturally, as circumstances change, priorities and objectives must change as well, but this should not occur too frequently. When someone vacillates, it is likely that they have never really sat down and thought through what they are trying to achieve, or how. Here, as in so many areas of management, time spent in formulating proper objectives and outline plans is amply repaid in time saved later on.

An allied problem is the manager to whom people are always turning to sort out problems of who should be doing what. Such problems arise when responsibilities are not clearly allocated in the first place. You can't tie everyone down too precisely in a small firm or section, and people must be prepared to share responsibilities and to stand in for one another, but that does not mean that chaos should be the order of the day.

COMMUNICATIONS AND DECISION-MAKING

There are also firms where there are frequent misunderstandings which have to be sorted out by the manager. Dealing with these on a one-off basis gives some managers a feeling of power and satisfaction. But such occurrences are warning signs of an underlying malaise: poor communications. Action needs to be taken to clarify the lines of communication and to improve people's skills, if need be, in this area. (Advice on this is given in Chapter 18.)

The old proverb about procrastination being the thief of time still holds true. While it is sound practice to collect relevant information and assess alternatives before taking decisions – if there is time – indecision is not sound management. Unless there are good reasons for deferring decisions, delay merely wastes valuable management time, as the arguments have to be rehearsed over and over again.

TASK ASSESSMENT

Another way in which thinking time is eroded is when the time taken to undertake a given task is grossly under-estimated. (Some managers seem to be born optimists, always saying, 'That won't take long'.) If you or one of your people behave like this, get them to start recording how long they consider tasks will take, and then comparing the results with their estimates. Hopefully, with practice and reviewing of results, they will learn to be more realistic.

CRISIS MANAGEMENT

When a crisis occurs, some managers seem to run around like beheaded chickens, going through the motions without any sensible decisions being made. Unless the individual is suffering from severe mental stress, such action probably indicates a lack of training and self-discipline. Managers who really understand the business they are in and the technology they are using should be able to tackle a crisis in a constructive manner, keeping one eye on the longer-term objectives of the firm while they sort out the immediate difficulty. One can expect that managers who do not know their business and its direction will be quickly thrown off course by unexpected occurrences.

SELF-MANAGEMENT

Most of the problems expressed above come down, in the end, to one key factor: self-management. If managers cannot manage their own time, paperwork and priorities, they are unlikely to be effective in getting results through the efforts of others. Each manager should have clear aims, consistent with the aims of the firm, a clear idea of how he or she will achieve these aims, and a system for monitoring progress and for managing the paperwork in support of these aims. Where teamwork is essential for success, these aims should be shared with other members of the team (see Chapter 12).

The likelihood is that if you and your colleagues take action along these lines in the priority areas for your operation, you may save yourself one or two hours per week. Some of this might well be spent on thinking and planning for the future. Many others have had this experience. If at all possible you should not attempt this alone, but in collaboration with colleagues.

PLANNING AND DELEGATION

Among the strategies outlined above for managing time, two stand out as of overriding importance in most cases: planning and delegation. Most managers know this, but they find it hard to put into practice; hence the need for the analysis tools already given. These will help you get things into perspective.

Planning simply means consciously sorting out priorities: devising objectives, time scales and action plans to achieve the objectives; and setting aside time to get the work done. Planning under pressure means that you will need to be ruthless about priorities. It often helps to classify the tasks you have before you into three kinds:

1. Must do
2. Should do
3. Ignore

Delegation means identifying those tasks you do that could, with a little coaching perhaps, be undertaken by your subordinates; and then letting them get on with the tasks assigned. Sensible delegation enriches the jobs of subordinates and releases the manager's time to deal with other matters. (It may even give him or her time to think!) The coaching that will be needed before you feel happy to leave some special responsibility with a subordinate may seem an expensive use of time at first, but generally speaking it is an investment that can pay handsome dividends.

ACTION GUIDELINES

1. Get your people to recognize the cost-value of time.
2. Get key people, including yourself, to identify where time is spent, and question the value of that expenditure.
3. Classify the way time is spent. Under each heading see how this can be used more profitably – or whether there are tasks that can be left undone or delegated to staff paid on a lower scale.
4. Be prepared to spend time in the short term (eg, in simplifying procedures, coaching staff to accept more responsibility) to give a pay-off later.

CHAPTER 12

Learning to Work Together

When a group of people work together in an effective manner, their output is more than just the sum of their individual efforts. Have you ever watched a group of people putting up a marquee? One method is to lay the tent out on the ground, insert the poles, stake the two end ropes and then pull on the ropes at the side, having someone ready to secure the ropes on the opposite side. The people who pull the tent up straight must work together.

Suppose you want to lay a pipeline in the North Sea. The pipe must be taken out and welded together piece by piece, on the ship, with the completed part of the pipe laying on the sea bed. If the pipe is just fed out on the back of the ship, it will snap. So two tugs have to be employed, coming up behind the ship with a strong wire stretched between them, to support the pipe at a suitable distance from the ship. For this exercise to work, the ship has to move forward fitfully, as each new piece of piping is welded on, and the two tugs must follow behind at the right distance. The people concerned must all work together. The important point about this illustration is that the decisions of the officer in charge of the ship depend on the actions of the welding team; and the decisions of the tugboat skippers depend on the speed and direction of the ship. Their work is interdependent.

Is that not true of so many aspects of your business? In a manufacturing operation, for example, decisions about production depend on the results achieved by the salespeople. This may depend, in part, on advertising, on the quality of your goods, or on the efficiency of your arrangements for despatching goods in response to orders. Decisions by your salespeople (eg, the extent to which different products are promoted) may depend on your productive capacity, and/or your ability to transport goods by a given time at a reasonable cost. It is important that these various aspects of a business keep in step.

On the other side, it is important that you maintain a sensible balance between the purchase of raw materials and their storage, in the light of the anticipated production requirements, and in relation to your proposed storage of finished goods. Maintaining stocks at an economic level requires more than making decisions about what stocks to keep. It is also a question of ensuring that all the people involved understand the arrangements and keep each other informed of any problems likely to emerge; as, for example, if sales rise more rapidly than anticipated. The people concerned must work together.

A potential source of friction is the tension between quality and output levels, especially if you polarize the issue by putting one person in charge of production and another in charge of quality. In some operations this may be the only way to make it work, but it is important to recognize and manage the conflict inherent in such an arrangement. The best way to do this is to help the people concerned recognize that they have, in fact, a shared goal: to produce the required quantities of the prescribed quality goods.

The important point is that, together, they have failed if the production output targets have not been met. They have also failed, together, if the quality is not good enough. Thus the production manager, in this situation, will be motivated to produce quality goods, and the quality officer will be motivated to help the production manager maintain production. Here, as in so many cases, effective teamwork is as much an attitude of mind as the ability to work with someone else.

If these two people are to collaborate, they must also know something about each other's tasks and problems on a day-to-day basis.

There are thus four key points to bear in mind if you are to get teamwork where you need it. These are:

1. Find the people who need to work together.
2. Identify and promote shared goals.
3. Help the team members learn to understand each other.
4. Help the team members learn how to interact with each other.

So much for the preamble. It is now time for you to get out your pen and do some work. You need to identify where teamwork really matters in your firm.

WHERE TEAMWORK MATTERS

A group of professional people in partnership (eg, doctors, solicitors or accountants) may find that for the bulk of their time they work individually with patients or clients. Thus, active collaboration between the partners in such a practice may be only rarely necessary. They must, of course, agree on such matters as the location of their surgeries or offices, and about the recruitment and deployment of their supporting staff, but teamwork, as such, may not be needed.

Apart from examples of this kind, the need for effective teamwork and collaboration between people in organizations, large and small, is often crucial to success. (Of course, in a hospital or in dealing with the accounts of very large client firms, effective collaboration between the professionals mentioned above will also be crucial.) Can you identify a particular group of people in your firm who must work together to be successful? That is, in what areas of the business are the decisions and actions of each person dependent upon, and likely to act upon, the decisions and actions of the other individuals concerned? Not one of them alone can deliver the goods. There may well be two or three groups of this kind.

This situation arises, as described in the example above, where activities are interlinked – like purchasing, with stores, sales and distribution in a manufacturing firm; or between production, maintenance and control. Effective liaison may also be required where items of production or information are passed from section to section, where what is being done in one section is helpful to another.

In a service organization, for example, where service engineers visit customers' premises to carry out maintenance and repairs; or where mobile car mechanics carry out roadside repairs; or where advisers visit companies to provide consultancy or training services, there is an essential need for effective collaboration between the central office receiving requests for visits, the people in the field, and subsequently the people who will file the reports and issue the invoices to clients.

In such a service operation, the manager needs periodic

information about the activities of the people in the field, and also quantitative and financial data about travelling expenditures, the average time taken per visit, etc. If this information is to be useful for monitoring purposes, it is important that the people who produce this data do so in a helpful form.

You can identify the need for teamwork if you can write down a statement of what is required in output terms (quality as well as quantity) and put down more than one person who can influence the activity in question in a marked way. If your company or section is big enough, there will be a group of directors or managers who need to work together, and any teambuilding work must start with this group.

SHARING GOALS

You will generally find it difficult to get people to work together if they see themselves as having different goals – even if these goals do not conflict. We have already cited the examples of the quality-versus-output problem. Here, an approach to a shared objective is to make both parties jointly responsible for achieving the output at the required level of quality.

Consider again the example of the manager of a field force of salespeople and the person who provides him or her with monitoring information (let's call him or her the finance officer). On the face of it, the finance officer is there to account for where the money comes from and how it is spent. There ends his or her responsibility. It is up to the manager to use the information provided as a tool; but that is a poor view of how things ought to be.

The finance officer should see him or herself as responsible for providing information which will help the sales manager to monitor the activities of the salespeople. Better still, the manager, the finance officer and the salespeople should see themselves as a team, aiming to use their time and expertise profitably: there is the shared objective. Understood in this way, we would expect to find a willingness on the part of the people in the field to provide the basic information; the finance officer willing to work out how to collaborate and present the data usefully; and the manager using the information provided in a sensible and sensitive manner.

Take another example. Suppose that for one reason or another an expensive machine is out of action for an undue proportion of working hours. It could be owing, for example, to frequent breakdowns, running out of raw materials or running out of storage space for finished materials produced. One of the problems here is that apart from the manager, and perhaps the machine operative, the people concerned may not realize the cost of machine down-time in terms of an under-used capital item. The maintenance fitter may simply see this as just another machine in need of repair. Those responsible for the supply of raw materials and the storage of finished goods may see this matter balanced off against some of their other priorities, and other demands on space, and so forth.

One approach to changing this situation is to bring the people together and get them to calculate the hourly cost of having the machine, even when it is not being used; and then to charge them, jointly, with the responsibility for reducing the machine down-time. They will then contribute their own ideas and suggestions as they get to know and understand each other's problems. Don't try to solve the problems for them: if they are competent at their jobs, they will probably come up with better answers than you would anyway, and they will certainly be keener to make their own ideas work than somebody else's.

Some ideas that might arise include a closer working relationship between the machine operator and the mechanic, where the operator notes carefully what happens as the machine's performance begins to deteriorate. This information could reduce the time taken by the mechanic in fault diagnosis, and hence reduce the time taken to effect a repair. Another idea might be that when the operator notices that storage space for products is taken up to an agreed level, he or she alerts the person responsible. Simple ideas – dependent on the local situation – but probably effective all the same: beware of a complicated solution when a simple one will do.

A word of caution. Make sure you have identified the problem and priorities correctly. If reducing the machine down-time is not the most critical factor, you have set people on a wild goose chase. Maybe you could let them look at how to minimize the cost of the overall operation.

Another illustration of where teamwork might be needed is where a company faces a high turnover of employees. You will need to look carefully at the information you have about when and why people leave, and then bring together all the people in the company who can make a difference. Suppose the turnover is in your packaging department: you will need to include in the discussion the people who carry out recruitment, induction and initial job training, the manager of the department and the boss who determines the pay and employment conditions.

This group of people will need to discuss such questions as whether the people being recruited are right for the job; whether the methods of advertising, interviewing and selection procedures convey the right picture; whether the pay levels, hours of work, and so on are competitive in the local labour market; whether the methods and pace of initial training and the way newcomers are treated is appropriate; whether people find difficulties in travelling to the site, and so forth. You will probably find that the most fruitful approach to the problem requires concerted action on the part of several people – teamwork. The shared goal could be a specific reduction in labour turnover within a specified period of time.

You can now set about looking for areas where learning to work together can be encouraged by giving people shared objectives. In effect, this is a form of on-the-job training, interwoven with the day-to-day life of the firm.

UNDERSTANDING EACH OTHER

On the face of it, you would expect people to understand each other when they talk. If you take the trouble to notice what is going on around you, however, you will find that this is not always the case. Often the same message has to be repeated several times, and still it is not acted upon. There are several reasons for this, and one of them is that people tend to interpret what is said in terms of their own knowledge and experience.

When you bring together a team of people with different backgrounds and experiences, communication problems of this kind are almost inevitable. An accountant looks at things differently from the technologist. Each will have a different set of values, a different view of what is important. They may use the same words in two different ways. If a team is to be effective, ways must be found to overcome these barriers to communication.

There is no doubt that discussions based on work problems help, especially if people are prepared to let each person explain how he or she sees the problem. If the problem is serious, there are training methods which can be employed, for example using role play, where one individual acts the part of another in seeking the solution to a problem or in doing some kind of exercise. Training courses of this type require experience to set up, however, and may be too expensive for the smaller firm. In larger firms there is merit in having these courses specially designed around the problems that need to be tackled.

Where two groups of people within an organization find it difficult to communicate or co-operate, there are methods which can be used based on the idea of getting each group to write down how they consider the other group behaves, and how they consider *they* are seen by the other group. These perceptions are then shared, and the problems so highlighted can be dealt with in a constructive manner. Leading such events, however, is not easy and experience is essential.

INTERACTING WITH EACH OTHER

When a group of people who need to work together evolve shared goals and learn to understand each other's points of view, they are well on the way to successful teamwork. The final piece in the jigsaw puzzle is to get people involved in 'effort bargains': 'If you do this for me, I'll do that for you'. In practice it is not as simple as that, but if people are to play their full part, what they need to know is what other members of the team expect from them by way of information and services, and what they can expect from each other.

There are a number of ways people can learn about this. One way to get started is to ask each person involved to get a sheet of paper ruled down the centre, and to put down the name of another team member and seek to answer two key questions (see Figure 21). Then repeat the exercise for another member of the team, and so forth. Finally, the sheets are compared. You may be surprised to find how many misapprehensions there are around. This may sound like a cumbersome approach, and one to be used sparingly, but it can prove helpful.

Figure 21 Teamwork

Team member's name and job title:______________________

What do I expect this team member to do for me in relation to the achievement of the team goals?	What does the team member expect me to do to help him or her in respect of the achievement of team goals?

Another approach, particularly suitable for newcomers, is for the individual concerned to spend a little time with each team member in turn and ask the two basic questions. This is far less formal and requires no paperwork. It is not as thorough as the other method, but it may suffice. As in every form of human endeavour at the workplace, the example and support of the boss, and praise when deserved, will help the process along.

ACTION GUIDELINES

1. Identify areas of work in the company where success depends on a group of people working effectively together. Don't forget the managing partners, the board of directors or the group of senior people who run the firm.
2. Help each of these groups to learn to be more effective by recognizing what their shared goals are.
3. Help members in each of these groups understand the roles, responsibilities and strengths of other team members.
4. Help team members master the art of communicating and collaborating effectively together.

CHAPTER 13

How People Learn

The first part of this book has been concerned mainly with recognizing how and where your company can benefit by increasing the knowledge and skills of its people. This part of the book is concerned with how this learning can be achieved.

It is said that people learn by experience. That is only half true. People learn when they review – ie, when they think over their experiences, rehearse them in their minds and try to make sense of them, seeking for links, connections and patterns. There must be some kind of reaction to each experience if significant learning is to take place. In some cases that reaction can be purely in the mind, without any outward manifestation that this has taken place. In most cases, however, learning is more effective when it is reinforced by some activity on the part of the learner.

It is also said that people develop skills through practice. This is also only half true. At each practice attempt, the learner must have a knowledge of the results, and will need to know how to modify the way he or she behaves at the next attempt, if necessary, to obtain a better result. Often help is needed (eg, as given by a coach in sport) if there is to be a real improvement in performance and not simply a repetition of incompetent behaviour. In other words, it is quite easy to keep on practising but making little progress, which is very discouraging.

When you read a newspaper, you read through some of the items slowly and carefully, taking in every word, whereas you skim through others quickly, so that even a few minutes afterwards you would find it difficult to recall much about the items which did not interest you. Most people are like that. It is only when they *react* to the items that significant learning takes place.

Have you ever been at a party when a lot of people are talking at once, as they are huddled in little groups? If someone in another group mentions your name, the likelihood is that suddenly you become aware of that particular conversation. Out of all the hubbub, most of us prick up our ears at this telltale signal; learning suddenly starts to occur as we strain to hear what someone is saying about us. This ability to ignore unwanted sounds and conversations and pick out the ones we consider important is sometimes known as the 'cocktail party problem'.

What these two illustrations have in common is that the interest has been captured, so that the mind reacts to the experience (of scanning a newspaper or hearing a conversation). Without that reaction, little learning occurs. In the context of workplace learning there are important lessons to be taken into account. For example, substitute for the newspaper a report that needs to be studied and absorbed; or for the party, a meeting where information has to be exchanged. These are two occasions where learning has to take place. In each case the interest and attention of the people who need to learn have to be captured.

This has important implications for the people in the organization who produce written work. They must learn how to write it in a way that captures the interest of the audience they are trying to reach (see Chapter 17). Similarly, people who lead meetings must learn how to conduct them in a way that commands the attention of those who attend. On the other side of the coin, those who read reports and documents, and those who attend meetings, need to learn the disciplines of reading and listening to gain understanding and retention of key facts and concepts.

So far we have focused on knowledge, and we have noted that skills are needed to impart this, and to acquire it. But the learning that people need to improve at work involves skills, understanding and attitudes as well as knowledge. Experiences through which people can learn occur almost everyday. Chapter 15 looks at one method – coaching – whereby selected experiences at the workplace can be used to help people to develop their knowledge and skills.

If you want to develop people's competence in the company context, you need to think about how to set up experiences for people whereby they can acquire the knowledge, understanding, skills and attitudes they need to be effective in their jobs. In each case it is worth thinking about the kinds of experience people need to acquire these, and how they can be helped to see the results of their work, to receive insights through these observations and to learn from the experiences and insights.

Although it is possible to make some general statements about how people learn, it is important to realize that people vary in their ability to learn, in how fast they learn and also in respect of which learning methods work better for them. Sometimes teachers and trainers have been guilty of saying that such-and-such a person can't learn how to do something, when the real failure is in the trainer's ability to discover and provide the appropriate learning experiences for the individual concerned.

Don't be too hasty and give up on someone who seems to be slow at first. If you can find the key that unlocks the obstacle to learning for that person, you may gain a very useful worker, and uncover hidden talent. Some people who learn slowly ultimately out-perform people who learn quickly – especially in work of a routine nature. Jobs the bright person can learn to do quickly may turn out to be boring to that person so that their performance deteriorates, rather than improves with time.

An experience most people receive at work is observing the boss and other workers in action. If people value what they see, they tend to follow the model. The power of a good example cannot be stressed too much. Conversely, the power of poor models (eg, a slapdash boss or senior craftsman) is very significant.

Figure 22 How people learn

Experience

Looking at diagrams, text, people, equipment, films, television, computer screens, printouts.
Listening to people, machines, lectures, audio tapes.
Touching materials, keyboards, instruments.
Tasting foods, wines.
Smelling foodstuffs, chemicals.
Sensing the reaction of a tool being applied to a machine or to a material.

Response

Mentally reacting to the stimulus of what is heard, seen, felt, smelt or tasted.

Replying to questions asked, having turned the problem over in the mind.

Adjusting behaviour in the light of information received.

Review

Seeking to make sense of the information gathered from various sources, trying to find connections or patterns and deciding what to do or try next.

Trials

Having a go at doing something in the light of information gathered from the sources mentioned above.

Having another go at something, doing it a little differently in the light of experience and the knowledge of the results of previous trials, possibly also with advice from a specialist.

GAINING SUBJECT KNOWLEDGE

Very few individuals have a 'photographic' memory. Such a person can read something in a journal or magazine, and years later recall the entire article, page by page, virtually word by word. Most of us would have to work very hard to remember even the main points for a few weeks let alone a few years. One of the problems with learning knowledge is how quickly we forget. Students have to revise for examinations, going over material that they studied perhaps several months before. On the positive side, revision is a cost-effective exercise: it takes far less time to re-learn something than to learn it from scratch for the first time.

It is useful to distinguish between knowledge which underlies daily work (eg, knowledge about electricity for the electrician, or about the layout of documents for the typist), and the specific knowledge required on the job (eg, the particular circuitry of the electrical apparatus designed by your firm, or the preferred layout for your company documents). Subject knowledge (eg, about electricity or document layout) can be acquired through reading textbooks or external courses, but knowledge about the equipment and procedures of the firm is generally best acquired through the workplace and the people who work there.

How can you and your people acquire the requisite subject knowledge? The obvious ways are to see it or hear it, or both. Some people find that they can get knowledge simply by reading, especially if the text is written in an interesting way, but most people find that some additional activity is necessary to stimulate a review of the information. They might try to recall the main points and summarize them in writing, for example, or try to answer some questions about what they have read. In some books (as in this one) there are questions and/or summaries at the end of each unit or chapter to aid this process.

Programmed learning texts work on the principle of providing small amounts of information and then inviting the reader to answer questions on each item before passing on. The modern version of this principle is embodied in computer programmes which require the user to respond to a question (eg, by pressing a key or touching the screen) before moving on to the next item. Programmes of this kind can provide a variety of responses according to the way the user answers the question. This is much easier with a computer than when a written textbook is used.

Provided the user finds using the programmed text or computer acceptable, these methods have several advantages. They enable the individual to learn at his or her own natural pace, with minimum supervision from anyone else. People who find it difficult to master the subject in question may find it helpful to have the material broken down into small portions. However, many people find the written programmed text boring after a while, but if this can be interspersed with other activity, like practical application of the knowledge or the use of other learning methods, programmed texts can be useful.

Once the initial apprehension about computers has worn off, many people find that tinkering with one is absorbing, so that learning programmes based on computers can prove highly effective. If you have a computer with spare capacity in terms of time and the ability to handle training software packages, it may be worth trying out some simple programmes. The problem is that often there will be difficulties in fitting the use of the computer for learning within the daily routine of the firm. Programmes can also be provided on microfiche, and if you have a viewer it might be worth enquiring about what texts are available, although at the time of writing these are not prolific.

Correspondence courses and other 'open learning' methods can be used to help people acquire subject knowledge, but the materials need to be well-produced, and the user keen to succeed. If you or your people embark on these, you will need a lot of encouragement and support. Open University courses are largely high-quality correspondence courses backed up by a nationwide network of tutors who can give local support, and by radio and television broadcasts. Opportunities are also provided for students to meet from time to time.

The main value of radio and television broadcasts is the stimulus they provide to learning, enabling students to pace themselves and also to listen to explanations and (in the case of television) to witness illustrations. Other ways in which listening can be used to enhance knowledge learning are with audio/video tapes, records and video discs. In some schemes, much use is made of the telephone or of closed-circuit television as a way of allowing students to interact with tutors.

Simply viewing films or video tapes has limited value in terms of acquiring knowledge: some form of reinforcement is needed if substantial knowledge is to be acquired. However, such methods can be useful in stimulating interest; and if they are used as the basis of group discussion, for example, a lot of knowledge learning can take place.

In recent years there have been considerable developments in the materials and support available to help people to learn in 'open' and flexible ways – using techniques which enable an individual to learn at his or her own pace and choice of location. Some of the materials and supporting systems provided are good, but many are not, so exercise care in choosing such materials. Be sure that the open learning material covers the right subject matter at the right level and that it is readily understood and attractive to the person who needs to learn.

So far only the learning of facts has been considered. Very occasionally there may be a need to memorize text. Many people find that there is really no substitute for reciting it over and over again. If you have easy access to a tape recorder, you can listen to what you recite and correct this against the master text until you get it right. Unlike mere acquisition of knowledge, learning text is a skill, and hence there is a need to have a feedback on performance if mastery is to be attained.

Some people find that it helps to have a pattern worked out for items to be memorized, and others find that some mental prop helps (eg, to remember the colours of the rainbow, thinking of 'Rows of Youngsters Gorging Beef in Vinegar': Red, Orange, Yellow, Green, Blue, Indigo and Violet). However, in crucial matters it is not good enough to rely on the memorization of text. If a series of checks are to be carried out (eg, in bringing a machine into operation) it is best to refer to a written checklist. It is not a virtue to rely on memory when a written list can be used.

The methods discussed so far could be used by someone entering the field for the first time, and wishing to gain knowledge in general about the subject. In one sense the person is like an empty vessel waiting to be filled with knowledge, but with one important difference: each person comes with a personal set of expectations and previous experiences. The problem is that, if time is short, a great deal of non-essential information will be absorbed along with the useful material. One way around this is to start off with a checklist of information to be acquired, and to set the learner off on an enquiry to discover the relevant facts (see, for example, the induction checklist in Figure 24 on page 117).

Methods like this which put the initiative with the individual learner rather than with the 'teacher' can be effective in the right situation. The individual must be able to get the information, for example, by going to a library or by interviewing people who have the knowledge. The process of extracting the knowledge from written material or by discussion with knowledgeable people is an effective learning method, so long as the person concerned is happy to use it. If you start someone on a project of this kind, getting them to discuss it with colleagues can be a way of reinforcing the learning for the individual, and also a way in which that learning can be shared within the firm. See Figure 23 (on page 116) for further ideas on gaining subject knowledge.

FIRM-SPECIFIC KNOWLEDGE

Often, the more immediate problem for a firm is how to get knowledge about the firm, its products, its equipment, its procedures, the raw materials handled, and so forth. Not everyone needs to know everything about the firm, and the earlier part of the book contains advice on how to decide what each individual should know.

Figure 23 Gaining knowledge

Knowledge can be acquired in a variety of ways. Choosing the most appropriate method depends on the type of knowledge that must be acquired and the preferred learning methods of the people concerned. This list should prompt you to consider alternative methods and to think of other approaches.

Method	*Comment on reaction*
Reading	mental response: interested?
Reading/summarizing	writing down summary or talking about it
Reading/answering questions	writing down answers talking about them responding to a programmed text responding to a computer programme responding to a microfiche programmed learning package
Feedback on answers	reinforcement through positive feedback; be careful of criticism
Listening to/watching tapes, discs, broadcast programmes, films	interest generated? support of a tutor? keeping pace? opportunity to discuss with colleagues?
Enquiry	use of checklist of information required

There is no need to panic about this, or to introduce sophisticated training methods to deal with frequently-occurring items. Most people will acquire the knowledge they need from each other and from your existing paperwork. The two areas you need to be careful about are the help given to newcomers (see Figure 24) and the steps which should be taken when any significant change occurs or is planned.

Figure 24 Induction checklist

What does the newcomer need to know and at what stage?

What is written down and what must be said?

Who will give the information?

Draw up your own list using the items below as a starting point.

The firm	History and organization. Products, services and markets.
Employment conditions	Pay rates, methods of payment, payslips. Overtime, holidays and other leave. Sickness, absence and certificates. Timekeeping and time recording methods. Contract of employment. Trade union membership. Grievances and disciplinary procedures. Terms of service (within first 13 weeks).
Starting procedure	Documents (eg, tax, birth certificate). Medical examination, if required. Protective clothing. Introductions to key people.
General information	Cloakrooms and washrooms. Meals, breaks and eating places. Welfare facilities and parking. Smoking. Security. Purchase discounts, if any.

Health and safety	Fire precautions and exits. Action in case of fire or bomb threats. Machine safety, tools and equipment. Good housekeeping and hygiene. Safety methods and first-aid arrangements.
Personal training plan	Covering the job itself.

Note: It is useful to arrange an interview after a few months to see how the newcomer is getting on.

DEVELOPING UNDERSTANDING

In essence, the kind of method described above for gaining knowledge can also be used to help people acquire understanding, but there will be some important differences in the way information is presented and questions are raised for the learner to consider. If understanding is to be developed, it is imperative that questions are posed which call for an appreciation of the processes involved or the relationships between different items.

This can often be reinforced by helping people to draw up decision-trees or algorithms which help them to think through the logical connections between various factors. Another method is to draw up schematic diagrams that illustrate a process – for example, a domestic plumbing diagram can be provided, and the trainee asked what would happen if some part of the diagram is changed (eg, a tap turned off, a pipe connected incorrectly, and so forth).

In training people to understand financial matters, one method that works with a very wide variety of people is to set them problems where, for example, budgets, cash flow projections or profit and loss forecasts must be prepared. Actually working through carefully prepared sheets, with the absolute minimum of explanation, doing the sums with pencil and paper or printing calculators actually works better for most people than listening to brilliant lectures or viewing colourful video-taped films.

Such work is helpfully supplemented and reinforced by good computer training programmes or relevant video-taped films if these are available.

ACQUIRING SKILLS

In talking about skills, people often say that practise makes perfect. That is only half true. Some people practise, and practise, and practise and never seem to improve much. Apart from practise there is a need to gain feedback on performance. If you were trying to improve your ability to putt a golf ball, it would be no use hitting the ball behind a screen so that you did not see where it went. You need the feedback of knowing what happened. Did it veer to the right or left, and by how much? If you miss, you want to do it a little differently next time to see if you can get a little closer.

Thus, three things are needed if you are to develop skills: practise, feedback and adjustment of your own behaviour in the light of that feedback. Here the 'experience' you need for learning is the practise, and the response you need is this feedback and adjustment. Having an expert to demonstrate the skill in the first place is most helpful, and having an expert coach to help you to improve is marvellous – if you can get it. But one of the most important factors is this – wanting to succeed.

Having a skill means being able to perform a task, and in industry and commerce we want people who undertake tasks consistently and competently, not just people who know about and understand things. Some of the skills upon which your firm depends for its success may be simple – like putting a letter in the right envelope; others may be complicated and difficult – like setting a lathe, balancing the accounts, typing a table full of numbers or pricing a contract for which you intend to submit a tender. Never forget that the simple skills are often as crucial for a firm as the complex ones. It is no good preparing a marvellous tender by the due date if it is sent to the wrong address. We use the term 'skills' whether we are talking about mental skills (like keyboard dexterity, panel-beating or joinery) or social skills (like selling, leading a discussion or coaching).

How do people become skilled? First of all, they need to get some idea about what to do to perform the task. In the case of manual skills, this is usually by watching someone else do it first or being shown by someone who knows how to do the task in question. Often it is helpful if the person who demonstrates the skill knows how to illustrate the key features of the task, and how to break it down into steps that the trainee can absorb. In some cases it may be possible to make a video recording of the manual task and show this to the trainee.

In the case of mental skills, it is mainly a question of making sure that the learner knows the essential steps and the framework involved in the task. This can often be represented in words and figures either in writing or on a computer screen. In the case of social skills, the key is to sensitize the person to what is involved when people interact together. A film can be used to start a discussion and open up the issues involved, but ultimately the people concerned need to experience social interaction themselves and reflect upon it.

Many skills are combinations of mental, manual and social skills. In every case there is a need to evoke a response to generate learning, but in the case of developing skills there is the special requirement of practise, feedback and adjustment. Specific examples of this will be given in Chapters 16 to 19.

DEVELOPING ATTITUDES

There are essentially two schools of thought about attitudes. Some people say that if you so arrange matters that people have to behave in a certain way (eg, maintain their working area in a spotlessly clean state), eventually their attitudes will change in line with that. In the example, people will regard it as normal and necessary to work in clean surroundings. According to the second school of thought, people would say that if you can change people's attitudes ('It is pleasant and necessary to work in a clean place') their behaviour will change accordingly.

In practice, you are well advised to consider both points of view. In other words, to follow the example a stage further, make it the rule that the premises and equipment must be kept clean (eg, in a laboratory or food-preparation area), and at the same time, make sure that people understand why this is important.

In dealing with attitudes you are dealing with what people believe. At first this seems to be somewhat intangible, but it is important. If you can't watch people all the time, but you want them to behave consistently in a certain way, you need to move to the position where they believe it is important, and will observe the correct behaviour at all times.

One of the most common areas where attitudes really matter is safety. You should move to a situation where people behave in a safe manner, not just because of the safety rules and procedures (although training in these is important), but because they want to do so, believing it is the right thing to do.

So how do we get people to believe that safety, hygiene, good housekeeping, and so forth are right? What may be even more difficult, how do we get people to believe that quality products and services, and the containment of costs, are right? This depends essentially on five things:

1. Knowledge of correct procedures, and ability to carry them out.
2. Knowledge of the reasons behind correct procedures and practices, such that the trained worker will know when deviation is possible while still attaining the best results.
3. The example set by the manager and by respected workers; what is sometimes called the 'culture' of the firm; 'the way we do things round here'.
4. The reinforcement of important messages through discussions, posters, safety competitions, quality drives, and so forth.
5. Support for these attitudes through the procedures and reward systems of the firm.

In essence, therefore, attitude training means being clear about the values (safety, quality, etc) that are concerned, ensuring that your procedures and reward systems are consistent with these, and ensuring that you and your key people set the right example and have the appropriate expectations about levels of conformity.

Then the formal training can be directed to ensuring that people can operate the procedures, and know why they are necessary. It is important to use discussion methods in helping people understand the purpose of procedures. Occasionally the discussions that take place may cause you to question your procedures. Be open-minded enough to consider any serious suggestions that come forward from your workforce in this way. They might have something very valuable to contribute.

Attitudes that change in one direction can easily change back again. That is why continued attention is necessary. Changing or acquiring attitudes is not a once-for-all matter.

ACTION GUIDELINES

1. If you want people to learn, first capture their interest.
2. Does the person concerned need to acquire knowledge, master a skill or develop an appropriate attitude? Remember

that different learning methods are required in each case.

3. Are you sure that the method you are using to help people learn is appropriate – to them, to the situation and to the type of learning involved?
4. Remember that to maintain a positive attitude (eg, towards product quality or safety) requires constant attention.

CHAPTER 14

MOTIVATION TO LEARN

It is not easy to get people to learn about a job, about new machines and procedures, and about health and safety precautions, if they're not really interested. People are not going to learn much about how to improve their performance and that of their section if they don't really care. (It may also be difficult, at times, to get people to use the skills they have to the full, but that is a different, though not unrelated, problem.)

If you want to be successful in developing an effective workforce, several basic questions must be addressed. How do you identify what people should know and be able to do? How do you encourage them to enter energetically into the business of learning? How do you ensure that the best methods to assist learning are used, and that the results are worthwhile?

In encouraging people to learn and develop we have to ask ourselves two distinct questions. First, how can we make it worthwhile for people to learn and develop at work? Second, how can we make the experience of learning rewarding in itself?

REWARDS FOR LEARNING

There is a problem in using the word 'reward'. You may immediately think in terms of payment by results or bonus systems, but these are simply ways of rewarding *performance*. Larger companies often use promotion to a higher-grade post as a means of rewarding.

There are other incentives which often have a more immediate effect in terms of making people keen to be successful in the workplace. In essence, that is the best kind of reward resulting from learning – a feeling that because of the learning you have become more successful at work. This idea is so important that you ought to spend a few minutes thinking about it in your context. Write down as many answers as you can to the question, 'I think that in my organization people get a sense of being rewarded and successful when . . .' Don't make a meal of this: just jot down a few words or phrases which will remind you of the idea you have in mind in each case. You will not get full value from the next few paragraphs if you have shirked this task.

People feel rewarded when they get a rise, make a bonus or get a full pay packet as a result of high output on a payment-by-results system. You probably had something about this in your list. There are other factors – often closer to the real work itself, that make people feel successful. For example, some people find a great deal of satisfaction in seeing the job finished, and done well. This sense of success is increased considerably when someone notices and gives an appropriate word of praise to the person concerned. Praise from the boss or from colleagues is particularly valuable – especially if the judgment and opinion of the person giving the praise are valued.

The shop assistant who has made a large sale and considers that the customer was well satisfied; the craftsman who has set up the lathe and watches the metal being fashioned to a high standard; the cashier who gets the cash balances and records to balance at the first attempt; the technical salesperson who clinches a complex deal – these people feel rewarded by the work they do. Be careful not to underestimate the power of job satisfaction. You can capitalize on this in your firm by ensuring that everybody shares this sense of pride and pleasure in seeing a job done well at all levels.

The desire to do a job well is a powerful incentive to learn. Conversely, if nobody cares about the quality of work and pleasing the customer, this severely diminishes any incentive to be trained or to seek to improve performance. You may say that the kind of job people do in your company does not give rise to satisfaction in that way. Are you sure? Is there nothing you can do about this?

One way of helping to counteract such a situation is to make sure that each person knows how his or her task fits into the overall pattern of things, and why the job is important. If the job is not important, why is it being done at all? Every job should be seen to contribute either to the services given to customers and the quality of your products, or to the efficient running of the firm, which is the essential underpinning of the work for customers. That being so, it should not be difficult to help each person to understand the value of their own work and to feel a sense of pride in it.

Closely allied to this idea is the notion of belonging to a team – preferably a successful one. This is highly rewarding to many people. If individuals can't see much tangible output from their job, they should at least be able to see the point of the section in which they work. If they feel involved and have a measure of camaraderie with their colleagues, they will want to be competent to make their contribution, and hence keen to learn. They will feel that ignorance and incompetence in the work setting are letting the side down. This is another attitude that should be encouraged: the idea of sharing success and contributing to it.

One of the areas in which you can help people feel that they share in contributing to successful work is the way you use information. People who are left in the dark feel like outsiders. Since they don't know what is going on, they can't really feel responsible for the outcome. Inform all your people about the market place; the kind of service and goods customers want from you; how each product is selling; what the customers like about your products; why you have to change designs to meet new customer preferences; and so forth. Information of this kind helps people feel that they are part of a dynamic company doing a worthwhile job. The nearer they feel to the customer, the better. This feeling will help make them keen to learn how to do a better job.

You can enhance this feeling of involvement even further by discussing future plans with your people, and perhaps seeking their ideas and suggestions. The nearer the proposed changes come to their own work, the better their suggestions are likely to be; but you may well be surprised at some valuable ideas that arise. Naturally the extent to which you can discuss future plans with your people depends on the kind of business you are in and the nature of the proposed changes, but many managers inform and consult too little – rarely too much. Don't ask yourself why you should consult people over this or that; instead, ask yourself if there is any good reason for not doing so.

Above all, don't forget that human beings are social animals. Each one of us takes account of the opinion of others. It is a strange person who does not welcome a word of praise – if it is both justified and sincerely meant. Unjustified and/or insincere praise is an insult. If you and your senior people set the tone of the place by being ready to recognize good work whenever it occurs, and to give appropriate, sincere praise, you will create a situation where people want to succeed, and want to learn to succeed.

In summary, people will be more eager to learn to succeed if they:

- see a job well done
- see how their work fits in and contributes to the firm's output
- sense that they belong to a successful team
- feel informed about the firm
- feel informed about the future
- are consulted about what will happen
- hear genuine praise
- sense that their work is valued
- consider that their efforts are adequately rewarded.

No doubt you can add more items to the list. How do these ideas match up to your workplace? Would you like to have a go at revising your list? Perhaps you could use this to spark off a discussion with your colleagues.

REWARDS WITHIN LEARNING

The way in which learning is organized should, to some extent, provide its own reward.

This means that learning, training, coaching, development, and so forth should not be a drudgery, but a pleasure. Let's be honest, however, and confess that this is not always possible. In some situations the only way to get people to learn things is to upset them a bit. It can be bad for the training business when the people make judgments about which trainer to use on the basis of whether the participants 'liked' the sessions, rather than on the basis of whether they actually learned anything. Beware of training which is little more than entertainment.

Just as with ordinary workaday tasks, the achievement (a well-typed letter, a well-set up lathe, etc) is to some extent rewarding, so too the achievement of a piece of learning ('I can do that now!', 'I understand that now!') should be the driving force in helping people to develop their knowledge, skills and understanding. This has some important implications for setting up learning experiences. In learning, as in other activities, the learner should be able to succeed with a little extra effort. Set the learning tasks too hard, and the learner switches off because he or she loses hope. Make the learning tasks too easy, and the learner becomes bored. Learning should be a constant challenge: to do a little better, to remember a little more, to perform the tasks a little more quickly; such that every step forward is an effort, but can be done.

When you encounter people with learning difficulties, but you feel that they can learn to perform the required tasks, given time, one approach you can try is to break the tasks down into smaller and smaller parts. One of the major advantages of this method is that achieving the performance of a task, however small, aids the motivation to learn. Adults, including young adults, need this kind of encouragement. Adults do not learn efficiently by making mistakes and being corrected. It is easier to remember one correct way of doing a task than it is to remember all the wrong ways that must be avoided. Thus, the best strategy is to devise training which makes for a series of successes, even if these have to be somewhat modest for some people at first.

The very mention of the word 'success' implies that the individual has feedback on performance, and is aware of the standards required for that particular task. This feedback involves more than saying that any particular performance is right or wrong. It means helping the person concerned to understand what 'right' and 'wrong' mean. Thus, a correct performance can be recognized, and when an incorrect decision or movement is made, the consequences are clear, and the likely way of doing the task correctly next time is indicated. In skilled work it is necessary to specify standards of performance, and in the training to set a series of standards which the learner can attain as he or she makes progress.

Learning to swim, ride a bicycle, drive a car and use a sewing machine are some common examples of acquiring skill. You know when you have succeeded in learning to swim or ride a bicycle because you can get to the other end of the swimming baths without getting a mouthful of water, or get to the end of the road without falling off the bicycle. Somewhat more complicated standards are needed before you can tell whether you are safe to drive a car on the road or to use a sewing machine to make garments at a reasonable speed and quality.

It often takes time for people to learn to perform skilled work at speed to acceptable standards, but this represents an investment in the future – for as long as the individual works for you. If you help each person to understand what he or she is doing and what contribution this makes to the overall operation of the firm, and if you take care to help the individual develop the skills and knowledge to do the job properly, you will have gone a long way towards gaining the enthusiastic support of your workforce.

THE LEARNING CLIMATE

Some plants and flowers need a warm, draught-free, moist atmosphere if they are to grow. In the same way, people in a company need an environment where a spirit of enquiry, a desire to learn and a drive to improve skills are regarded as a normal and desirable state of affairs. People need to work in an atmosphere where thinking and talking through how to improve matters, learning new skills, and coaching a subordinate or fellow worker are all regarded as a legitimate and worthwhile investment of time. Senior people need to believe and demonstrate that they are in accord with these values if your firm is to develop the potential of its workforce – especially its managers – to the full.

ACTION GUIDELINES

1. How far can you structure jobs so that people can see the results of their efforts and how these fit into the overall activity of the firm?
2. How much information-giving and consultation do you need to give people a feeling of involvement in the firm's fortunes and sense of belonging to a winning team?
3. How often do you make the effort to give genuine praise for jobs well done, and encourage other people to do the same?
4. Can you set up learning opportunities that will be rewarding in themselves, such that the people concerned can succeed – with effort?

5. Can you create a climate in which the desire to learn, and to spend time doing it, is regarded as normal, healthy and desirable?

CHAPTER 15

COACHING AND WORKING

Much of the knowledge and many of the skills required to make your firm effective are already possessed by senior people – by you and the people who have built up the business. Your success is highly dependent on key decisions within the firm, decisions which in turn depend on the experience and judgment of this select group of people. The problem is, how can you ensure that this knowledge and experience and these skills are passed on to other employees, and that this level of maturity and soundness of judgment is exercised throughout the organization?

The answer is obvious. You and your senior colleagues must help your existing employees and newcomers to acquire these abilities through coaching as the work of the firm proceeds. Coaching is not something separate from work, it is a process that can really take place only while work is in progress. It may not always look that way, but think about it.

Suppose you take a supervisor aside to chat through how he or she might tackle the reallocation of duties to people when a new machine is introduced. He or she is away from the factory floor, being 'coached' – helped to make better decisions by talking it through. But has work stopped? Of course not. The supervisor's job involves thinking through how to allocate duties in a sensible way. He or she is working and learning at the same time. In the short run, coaching may seem to take a little longer than just telling people what to do and to get on with it. In the long run, it will save the firm a good deal of time as people become competent at their jobs, make better decisions and fewer mistakes, and leave senior people more time to do their own jobs.

We are accustomed to use the term 'coaching' in relation to sporting activities. Here, the acquisition of skills is part of the job of a professional sportsman or sportswoman. But coaching occurs when the man or woman learning the skills of the sport performs tasks, with the coach providing feedback information and guidance, and asking key questions, using his or her experience to help the learner to acquire an understanding of how performance can be improved. Remember that skills are as much in the mind as in the hand, foot and eye.

If you fail to coach people, you will either have to take all the key decisions yourself, or delegate decisions in the certain knowledge that many of them will be of poor quality – to the detriment of your firm. Trying to take every decision yourself will severely limit the size of your operation, and limit your ability to find time to look ahead and plan for the future. If the skilled people in your organization do not pass on their knowledge and skills to newcomers through coaching, how will they learn?

However, don't run away with the idea that coaching is only for others. If your colleagues have knowledge or skills that you would like to acquire, be humble enough to accept coaching from them. You may also belong to a business club of some kind, and you will, no doubt, be able to find there a trustworthy person who has knowledge and skills different from your own – but useful to you. You might consider a kind of deal with him or her whereby you exchange knowledge and talk through decisions that have to be made. If you each use this exchange to tackle real problems as you encounter them, you will be learning and working at the same time – you will be coaching each other.

Whether you are giving or receiving coaching, it is as well to know something about what makes this process work effectively. You might at this point be asking what all the fuss is about – you already pass on your knowledge and experience, so what's new? Have a crack at scoring your firm in terms of coaching: complete Figure 25 (on page 133). If you and your people are all good at helping each other learn through the practical everyday problems of working life, then what follows may not add much to your effectiveness. But if there is a chance that you could and might improve, it's worth reading on.

Two final comments before we get to grips with the art of coaching. First, if the people doing the coaching are incompetent at their job you are not going to get very far. Second, if you don't take it seriously, don't be surprised if nobody else does. What you need to encourage is an organization in which individuals are ready to help colleagues to learn, and where everyone is prepared to learn from each other.

LEARNING BY DOING – WITH HELP

Coaching is all about helping someone else learn from experiences and challenges. In sport, the coach demonstrates the task (serving the ball, say), invites the learner to have a go, and then points out the ways the action has to be modified to gain success. A good coach brings the learner on, step by step, building success on success. When the learner prepares to play (eg, in a competition) the coach will discuss strategy, how the game should be played in the light of the strengths and weaknesses of the opponent(s), the state of the court, and so forth.

The point about coaching is that, once the basics have been mastered, it is concerned with doing the activity and learning at the same time, and with preparing to meet new challenges. So it is with coaching at the workplace. It is concerned with helping someone who is actually doing the job by discussing how it could be improved, and helping him or her to prepare for new challenges by considering how new tasks might be undertaken. A large part of management coaching is concerned with helping the individuals concerned think through their objectives; consider alternative ways of achieving them; consider the resources at their disposal and the obstacles they are likely to face. Discussions like this build understanding and judgment.

In managerial coaching you should avoid giving solutions to problems as far as possible, and get the individuals concerned to think through the answers for themselves. Naturally, if you have a crisis on your hands, dealing with this takes precedence over coaching and you are wise to take prompt, decisive action. Remember, however, that if you solve all the problems rather than helping your manager to solve them, you gain time now, but later you will lose time by having to solve a similar problem because your manager has not acquired that skill. Coaching means spending time helping your people to improve; you gain time later by letting them get on with their jobs.

Coaching is an activity which arises from looking at the job in a certain way. It is not a 'formula'. Effective coaching at the workplace depends on managers who:

- genuinely want other people to develop and improve their skills
- use opportunities for coaching based on daily work
- encourage people to put forward their suggestions
- listen to other people's ideas
- ask questions in a way that encourages people to think through their ideas and follow them through, where appropriate
- check frequently to make sure that people understand what is being said and proposed
- open up the way for others to seek information and look into things for themselves
- reach agreements with people about the objectives to be achieved, and carefully review progress towards these.

You could use this list to assess your own degree of commitment to coaching. Another way of using the list is to get some of your managers to discuss the points raised, and where they might be applied in your firm. Figure 25 has these points arranged in the form of a questionnaire. If you get some key people to answer this (anonymously, if they are coy) and then tot up the results, you will have some data to discuss, and no doubt some areas for improvement will be highlighted. Another way to get coaching moving in your firm is to start a discussion based on the points in Figure 26 (on page 135).

Figure 25 Firm's coaching score

For each of the items listed below, circle *3* if the statement is consistently true, *2* if the statement is only partly true, and *1* if the statement is only rarely true.

Senior people in the firm are eager to help others to develop their abilities to the full.	3	2	1

Senior people in the firm often recognize and use opportunities that arise out of normal work to help their people improve performance. 3 2 1

Senior people in the firm encourage their people to put forward ideas and listen to what they have to say. 3 2 1

Senior people in the firm are seen to take into account the ideas put forward to them by their people. 3 2 1

Senior people in the firm ask questions in ways that enable their people to think through their ideas, and to explore solutions to work problems. 3 2 1

Having given instructions, senior people in the firm generally check to see that these have been fully understood. 3 2 1

Senior people in the firm encourage their people to seek information and help from others, and pave the way for them. 3 2 1

Senior people in the firm agree with their people about performance improvement objectives, and review progress with them from time to time. 3 2 1

Note A score of less than 20 leaves a lot of room for improvement.

As mentioned above, although it is common to talk about coaching one's subordinates, it is often helpful for people at the same level to coach each other where one has an area of expertise that could be useful to the other. If as a manager you feel secure, there is nothing to stop you from learning from your subordinates, and getting them to coach you in a topic where they have specialist knowledge and skills of value to you.

Figure 26 Hints on coaching

Learning by doing	Coaching is about helping people to do their jobs better while they are doing them. You can learn something about coaching by reading this chapter, but you learn to coach people only by doing it.
Aims for learning	Look for areas where improvement in performance is both possible and important. Discuss with the people concerned how improvements might be achieved. Agree on definite objectives, but don't be over-concerned with numerical measures – unless they accurately reflect the improvement you seek. Review progress towards these objectives with the people concerned at reasonable intervals.
Reinforcement and praise	Remember that people learn better by being encouraged when they succeed than by being castigated when they fail. This means giving correction before mistakes are made whenever possible, and giving praise when it is justified.
Learning by review	Remember that people learn when they react and respond to what is happening. Capture their interest – and show interest in them and their ideas. Ask questions that will stimulate people to think about the results of different kinds of action they might take.

Learning from mistakes

Look to the future. Remember that looking into things that go wrong should be an exercise designed to prevent recurrence – not to find and punish scapegoats.

Focus attention on what happened and why, not on who was responsible. If an individual made a wrong decision, explore whether this was the result of some factor which can be reduced (eg, fatigue, a misunderstanding or lack of training).

Learning by discovery

People can learn effectively by finding things out for themselves. Talking through with people what they need to know and how they can improve their performance can be a powerful form of coaching.

To be fully effective you need to think through, with people, a sensible series of steps in the learning process. It is no good trying to run until you can walk.

Choosing an interview style

In general, an open, constructive, forward-looking discussion works best.

A more aggressive style may be appropriate where a person is complacent, or not prepared to analyze the problem or the consequences of alternative actions.

It is rarely helpful, however, to end a discussion on a contentious note, unless there will be another opportunity soon to work towards agreement on positive aims.

On the basis of what style is appropriate, be prepared to vary your approach during the discussion.

ACTION GUIDELINES

1. Write down the areas of knowledge and skill in your business that can best be passed on by coaching on the job.
2. Determine how good your firm is at using the skills of its senior people to develop the skills of subordinates and colleagues.
3. Create interest in the value of coaching at the workplace, and set an example.
4. Be prepared to learn from other people who can coach you.

CHAPTER 16

Developing Practical Skills

Most industrial and commercial operations involve practical activities (eg, assembling a piece of machinery, typing a letter, setting up a capstan lathe, packing goods for despatch or operating a leather-cutting machine). Where such activities have to be carried out to a high standard, or where speed is essential, you need to think carefully about how the skills are acquired by the workers concerned. It is simply not good enough, in such cases, to show a worker a task and leave him or her to discover how to do the job properly and quickly. Whatever the job, you must ensure that all the safety aspects are covered in the initial training you provide.

There is now hard evidence that in many activities of this kind costs can be saved by training the people concerned, provided the training is properly done and you retain the services of those who are trained. Such savings arise because the cost of the training is more than offset by two factors: quality of work and quantity of output from the trained worker. Properly trained workers produce better quality work, and in many operations this will result in fewer defective goods being produced and fewer mistakes being made. In many operations the output of work of satisfactory quality from trained workers far exceeds that produced by untrained workers, especially in the early days of their employment on the tasks concerned. No doubt you can prove it for yourself by measuring the improvements when work is undertaken by properly trained people in your firm.

In the case of comparatively simple jobs, you may be able to undertake the necessary analysis and design of training yourself, but in the more complex operations you will need either to enlist the help of a specialist, or to arrange for one of your senior people to take a course on task analysis and training design. A simple explanation of the principles involved is given below.

PRACTICAL WORK

Many years ago, considerable numbers of people in industry were employed on purely manual work (ie, they used only their hands to do tasks like wrapping and packing or simple assembly jobs). Much of this work, especially where it is routine in nature, has been taken over by machines, but there are still occasions (eg, in the smaller firm, or with delicate work) where such tasks still have to be done by hand. If speed is not critical, extensive training is not called for, and simple instructions in the most important aspects of the job – security of the package, any safety precautions, and so forth – are probably all that is required. Often these operations are not routine in the smaller firm.

For many operations it is helpful to provide 'job aids'. These may consist of a simple set of instructions to inform the user, step by step, how to start up and operate a machine. Many office machines lend themselves to this. Take a simple photocopier, for example. A step-by-step set of instructions, accompanied by suitable diagrams, may be all that is required to enable an individual to use the machine, after that person is shown the different parts of the machine – where the control knobs, etc are located, what safety precautions must be observed and how to get help if the machine goes wrong. In such cases there is no need for the supervisor to trudge painfully through each step. If there is a particular knack needed (eg, if the paper has to be inserted with special care), this should be demonstrated.

There are some routine tasks that look very simple – for example, stuffing three items into an envelope and sealing it. If this task has to be done three or four times a day, there's not much training required. But if you want two people to stuff several thousand envelopes and seal them, you need to consider some system, where the piles of different items for enclosure and the envelopes are placed, and a sequence of actions that will ensure the efficient use of time and energy. The way the envelope is held, opened and closed, and the way each item to be enclosed is folded and put with the other items – all this becomes important.

Some practical tasks are so complex that it is not sensible to try to teach them on the job, where the learner is likely to hold up production. Jobs like filleting fish by hand, pattern-packing mixed pickles, assembling electrical or mechanical items are, generally speaking, best taught step by step at work stations separate from the full-speed operations. Competently undertaken off-the-job training of this kind is cost-effective.

Keyboard skills are almost invariably taught away from the job. Shorthand is much more than a manual skill and involves, in effect, learning a language as well as a script. Typing is also more than keyboard skills, as it includes such matters as layout and tabulation, and often the typist is expected to be able to spell and to recognize incorrect syntax. Nowadays, with the widespread introduction of computers and word processors, even more knowledge and skills are required by most people who use keyboards.

If practical tasks like assembly work are a regular part of your routine, you probably have got this all worked out, and the need is to train newcomers to operate effectively. If you are doing it for the first time, there is merit in talking to the people who will do it, and evolving and agreeing a sequence with them. The advantages of having these discussions are that (a) they will help to motivate the staff to do a good job, (b) staff will have faith in the methods adopted, (c) they are likely to suggest good procedures as they are close to the problem and (d) they will be on the look-out for improvements in procedures, knowing what they want to achieve.

Practical work can often involve the use of all five senses. Co-ordination between the signals received through these senses and the response of the person (eg, in terms of decisions and actions) is what skills are all about.

However, if there is a need to perform routine operations of this sort, and if sound procedures are in use, the problem is how, cost-effectively and quickly, to enable each newcomer to reach the required speed and standard of performance. This is of value not only to the company, but also to the workers concerned. It is disheartening to be left to do a job without proper instructions or the skills to perform satisfactorily. People like to succeed at any job, not to look slow and incompetent. A lot of labour turnover has been attributed to inadequate initial instruction and training.

There are many non-routine practical tasks where training is crucial, because the tasks themselves are critical to a firm's performance. Many machines that produce materials in high volume have to be set up at the beginning of a run and/or monitored and adjusted while they are running (eg, print runs or wire manufacture). Making observations and taking readings with sensors of various kinds, interpreting what these readings mean and making the necessary adjustments are crucial, and without proper training this becomes a hit-and-miss affair.

KEY TRAINING POINTS

What is distinctive about the actions of skilled and experienced workers, as opposed to learners, is not primarily the particular movements they make, nor the speed of these movements. The difference lies mainly in the manner in which they use their senses to derive information from the task and to control these movements. Learning the sequence of actions needed to perform a task is less difficult than acquiring the perceptual skills required.

Thus, the learner has first to master the sequence and a pattern of movements to achieve the task. Then the individual must learn how to sense what is happening and respond appropriately by initiating each movement, controlling it and bringing it to an end. To succeed, the trainee must learn where the information is coming from, how he or she senses it, and what to make of the messages he or she receives in each case. In the case of manual skills, much of this sensing, interpretation and response is not in terms of words and figures, or even mental pictures; but patterns are, nevertheless, built up in the mind.

When a carpenter gently pushes a chisel along a piece of wood, he or she is not only visually observing where the cut is being made, but is sensing, through the hand on the chisel, the energy he or she must use and the resistance being offered by the wood, and adjusting the force being applied appropriately. This feeling of the pressure exerted by the muscle through the hand is an example of the sixth sense – kinaesthesia – which is so important in many aspects of skilled work.

If the task is complicated, it is best to split the training into parts. Break the task down into distinct steps. Instruct the learner in each step in turn, giving the trainee the opportunity to practise each step and become competent at it. This involves helping the trainee, after each attempt, to recognize what improvement is needed and how this can be achieved.

During this process, the trainee should be developing skills in sensing what is happening and adjusting his or her actions in the light of these 'signals'. The acquisition of skill is all about developing this sensing ability and the associated actions through practise coupled with a knowledge of the results of each try, and with help on how to improve performance at the next attempt. If the materials used are valuable, the equipment expensive or the process hazardous, you cannot have a training procedure which wastes costly materials or permits potentially dangerous failures to occur. Here you will need to provide some activity which simulates the work task, so that the trainee becomes proficient and capable of safe working procedures before tackling the real thing.

In summary, to enable an individual to acquire the ability to perform a complicated, skilled task:

- ensure that the procedure for performing the task is efficient and safe
- explain the overall task and why it is performed
- break down the task into separate steps
- demonstrate each step to the learner, pointing out any efficiency features, like the angle at which a tool should be pushed, and any safety features, like the way a tool should be held or the correct position of the guard
- provide a job aid, if appropriate
- for each step, get the trainee to attempt the sub-task and to observe the result
- for each try, ensure the trainee recognizes the extent of success and the nature of any faults
- for each try, ensure the trainee understands what kind of adjustment will bring about improvements at the next attempt
- get the trainee to practise the step until proficiency is obtained, before moving on to the next step.

When training in this way, it is important to avoid boring the trainee, so a variety of training aids and methods should be used. For example, in training a mechanic to change the settings on a complicated piece of machinery, it might be possible to intersperse a video tape of the next step with references to the workshop manual and practical exercises on the machine.

VERSATILITY

Nowadays it is unlikely that the practical tasks people are trained to do will remain unchanged. Sewing machinists, for example, must be able to deal with not one but a range of garments and a variety of materials. Those with keyboard skills may be required to operate a variety of typewriters, computer terminals and software packages. Those concerned with assembling electrical or mechanical equipment will need to cope with a variety of products. To avoid the cost of retraining such workers from scratch each time a new product is to be made, it is well worth ensuring that the initial training imparts versatility, and that the 'culture' of the firm encourages people to recognize when skills they have acquired in one situation can be used in another.

The key points to bear in mind when workers need to be versatile are:

- ensure that your training methods motivate the learner
- match the training methods to the learning needs (eg, practise with feedback to master a manual skill, together with appropriate methods for acquiring the requisite knowledge)
- employ methods which build up the learner's ability to sense relationships and patterns in the work in hand
- provide opportunities for people to recognize how skills acquired in one situation can be applied elsewhere
- foster a readiness on the part of the learner to be prepared to use new skills in new situations, to learn new knowledge and to build new skills.

The need for learners to build up their sense of relationships is more subtle than many other needs, but essential if they are to be really versatile. One way of doing this is called the 'discovery method'. Here trainees have to solve, without aid from the instructor, a series of simple problems. They can proceed to the next problem only when the first one has been completed. The instructor is present in the background, ready to provide help if learners really get stuck. Learners proceed at their own pace, and most people find this approach more interesting and satisfying than being shown and told what to do. The sequence of problems has to be designed carefully, however, if it is to work properly.

In a process of this kind, people learn the easier tasks first, and build up knowledge gradually. They acquire practice and confidence in using new skills. They find things out for themselves from diagrams, simple instruction sheets and practical work. Instructions from a trainer or supervisor are kept to a minimum, because trainees learn more by working things out for themselves.

The supervisor or trainer is there to answer questions if necessary, and to help learners discover how things relate together and work. People who learn in this way generally retain their skills and can use them later. Moreover, when they are confronted with related tasks they adapt more readily to them.

Versatile workers have a range of skills that they can deploy to meet changing demands. Thus, if you want a versatile workforce, you will need to consider – for a given kind of operation – what the basic skills are. Then you will need to ensure that the worker learns these. For example, a sewing machinist needs to know how to use each part/attachment on the sewing machine and when to use them, and what seams and stitches to use for a particular purpose. As another example, a secretary using a word processor will need to know about each menu and programme, and the facilities of the hardware and software being used.

Even when people have skills which can be used in other situations, there is often a reluctance to try them out. Why is this? Generally speaking, people are a bit afraid of not being able to succeed in the new situation. If they feel that when they do try they will be ridiculed or abused if they get it wrong, this acts as a barrier to versatility. As a manager, you need to make sure that when people who try things out fail, their efforts are valued, and they are helped and encouraged to succeed. As far as possible, let people try out new skills without an audience. A crowd of onlookers does not help when you are trying to apply a skill in a new situation.

ACTION GUIDELINES

1. Identify the practical tasks where training will give a positive pay-off.
2. Decide whether the training is best given on the job or away from the pressures of production.
3. Set about designing appropriate training programmes and, where these would be helpful, job aids.
4. Use reliable external training resources where complex skills must be acquired.
5. Be careful to use discovery methods and the like when you seek to train your people to be versatile.

CHAPTER 17

DEVELOPING WRITING SKILLS

From time to time every entrepreneur and manager has to write – to compose letters, advertisements, tenders, and so forth. Often this is not a demanding task, but occasionally the ability to write in a concise and compelling manner is important, for example in writing reports, articles for publication, applications for loans or advertising material.

How can you and your people improve your ability to write such material? Good writing depends on having a clear message to convey, a sound structure for the written material, and on the use of appropriate vocabulary and sentence construction. If learning how to write well is a significant need in your organization, there are simple books on the subject to get you started, and there are short courses and correspondence courses which can be followed. Before you embark on a course, however, first be clear about the type of writing that matters to your firm or to your specific department, and make sure that this is covered adequately on the course.

In seeking to improve writing skills, there is really no substitute for coaching by somebody who can write well. This can be done by correspondence, but it is better face to face. What the would-be writer needs is sound, constructive criticism of his or her efforts, and advice on how to define the message, structure the material, choose the right words, sentence length, and so forth, and how to make the written work interesting to read, and readily understood by the intended audience.

PUTTING IDEAS INTO WORDS

Someone who wishes to improve their writing skills should be encouraged to spend time, before writing a significant document, in thinking through:

- To whom is this document addressed?
- What do I want to say?
- How do I want the reader to respond?

TO WHOM?

In the case of a simple document like a letter or memorandum, this preparation hardly needs to be written down, although the discipline is valuable and takes only a few seconds. The problem is that, if this step is ignored, it is difficult to check through the finished document to see if it meets the required standard. In developing writing skills, as in all learning, it is important to review what has been done, and to seek ways to improve.

If the letter or note is intended for a specialist in a particular subject, then you can use technical terms and expect them to be understood. If you are writing about some technical matter for a non-specialist, however, you cannot assume that technical terms will be understood, and you will need to ensure that any such words or phrases used are fully explained. This is particularly true of abbreviations, which now seem to abound in business correspondence, official documents and serious newspapers. Ask yourself whether the person to whom the letter is addressed is familiar with the abbreviations and expressions you employ.

If you are writing a more substantial document, perhaps an article for publication in a journal, or copy to be used in advertising material, the matter must be considered carefully. To take the journal first, you should read and study a number of issues. Try to form a precise image of the people who read this particular journal. There are plenty of clues. To whom will the main articles appeal? What sort of people buy the books and materials advertised in the journal? What interests these people will give you a lead on the subject matter of your article and its presentation.

If you are a manufacturer of small rowing boats, for example, you may wish to offer an article to a boating magazine. There are several of these, and by studying each journal in turn you may find one where the readers own large yachts – people who might be interested in a small boat to use for rowing in the harbour. Another magazine may deal with canals and river boats. Articles about your rowing boat should be different for the two magazines, and any photographs used should be appropriate.

Apart from the readership of a magazine, you must also consider editorial policy. How long are the articles as a rule? Are they typically racy, anecdotal and light-hearted, or serious and well-argued? There's no point in submitting a solemn 3,000-word article to a magazine that never publishes articles above 2,000 words and sets out to entertain rather than educate its readers. This may seem a simple message, but many people who start writing forget it.

It may be more difficult to gain a clear picture of the people you want to read some advertising material, for example, a leaflet for distribution at an exhibition, but the same kind of thinking is needed. If you study carefully the way the exhibition is advertised, this should tell you a great deal about the people who will attend. Take a machinery exhibition, for example. What sort of machines are being exhibited, and what kind of people are likely to be interested in seeing them?

If you are writing for young people or people with limited educational attainments, it may be necessary to consider reading age, and to edit your material accordingly. In general terms, the secret here is to use short sentences and short, commonly used words.

THE MESSAGE

On the face of it this might seem to be a simple matter, but all too often when people get down to writing a business letter or memorandum they don't know how to start and they can't seem to keep it short. If you have trouble starting, get out a piece of scrap paper and jot down in your own words, without worrying about good sentences or grammar, just what message you want to convey. Then ask yourself how you would react to this message. Then think of the person/people to whom the letter is addressed. How are they likely to react? This should give you some clues as to whether you need to either put it in simple words (if it is complicated), introduce it gently (if it is likely to be distasteful) or put it concisely (eg, if it is a simple and straightforward business matter).

What is the nature of the message? Are you merely giving information? Do you expect a response (eg, are you seeking information or an order)? If you are expecting a response, why do you think the recipient will give you one? What benefit do they receive? You may need to make clear the benefits of responding. Considering matters like this will enable you to make decisions about what needs to be said – the key points to be covered – and in what order. Publicity matter, for example, needs to start with something that commands attention. If a response is required, the letter, memorandum or leaflet needs to close with an invitation or request. Will some illustrations or examples help to put the message across, or make it more convincing?

STRUCTURE

In setting about the writing, having done the preliminary rough draft referred to above and set out the main points in order, it is often better to write quickly, not worrying too much about grammar and spelling to begin with, to gain the flow of ideas in the text. Then you will need to edit the document. Remember that most people find long sentences confusing: break them up into short ones. Use short words if you are writing for the general public or to people who are unfamiliar with the subject matter. You can happily use long words and jargon when you are writing for specialists – where jargon performs a valuable function in expressing the matter precisely and concisely.

When setting out the document you must be careful how you begin, how you develop the message and how you conclude. Remember that you are communicating with people, not machines, so the emotional reactions they might have must be taken into account. If you are trying to make a sale, or simply to commend your products, you are appealing to people's emotions as well as to their intellects. Even if your product is better than the next firm's, the buyer will choose the other one if he or she *wants* to do so, however powerful the arguments in your favour might be.

When you begin, try to capture the reader's interest, attention and, where appropriate, goodwill. As you develop the theme, make sure it follows a logical sequence, and one that will make sense to the reader. If it is a complicated matter, be sure the main points are summarized near the end. Close with a statement which makes it clear what you expect to happen next. Some examples of this are:

> 'Please let me know what you think of these proposals. Can you let me have a reply within ten days?'

'I would be glad to receive written confirmation of your order for ten machines along the lines that we discussed.'

'When you have had time to study this report, I will telephone you to make an appointment to discuss it.'

'I shall expect you to implement the new procedures by next Friday. Let me know if you foresee any problems.'

'I trust that you now understand the position. If not, please feel free to telephone me and I will seek to explain any outstanding points.'

All this may seem a laborious procedure, and clearly you do not need to do all this for every short letter or note. For the important letters, however, and for reports, advertising material, and so forth, taking time to form good habits will be amply repaid in the clarity and effectiveness of your written communications – thus enhancing the profitability of your business. This applies to you and to all the people in your firm who have to write for others.

REVIEWING/IMPROVING DOCUMENTS

Although individuals can do a great deal to help themselves by considering the matter referred to above, possibly with the aid of a textbook, progress will be much faster if key documents are discussed with colleagues. You might, for a start, get out some of the documents recently produced with your firm and discuss to what extent they meet the requirements set out above. A short discussion, perhaps using the questions below, should help those who take part to think constructively about how they can improve their own writing skills. The key questions about a document are:

- Will it be readily understood by the people for whom it is intended?
- Is the message clear?
- Is the opening appropriate (courteous, compelling)?
- Is the structure straightforward and logical?
- Is the language used appropriate to the readers?

- Are the examples and illustrations used (if any) apt, and do they reinforce or make the message clear?
- Does the ending make clear what is to happen next, and who is expected to take action?

Where a document is long and complicated, and intended for a busy senior person, it is imperative to produce a one-page summary of the key points, and to put this at the front. A busy person will not read past the first page unless he or she is convinced that the effort will be worthwhile. The cover page must be designed to compel attention, so that the reader wants to know how these facts were established and these conclusions drawn.

LEARNING TO IMPROVE

Good writers have developed the routines of planning, scanning and revising their documents. Thus, helping people to learn how to produce more effective documents should focus on these three areas. Planning means setting out a suitable structure, as discussed above. Improvements in structure can often result from a discussion with colleagues. Why not make a draft, from time to time, and discuss it with one or two people before you finalize the document?

If you know someone who writes well, or is knowledgeable about the subject, they will often be prepared to read through your first rough draft and make suggestions for improvement. You are not compelled to take the advice they give, but generally there will be some helpful suggestions. This will help you, not only with the document at hand, but also with the general improvement in your skills as a writer. It is another example of coaching.

Writers also need to learn how to scan draft documents they have written before editing them. This scanning is crucial in dealing with a longer document where it would be easy to edit a part of it in a way that diminished the overall impact. Scanning enables the author to maintain an overview of the whole report or article. Scanning means reading the document very fast to gain a feel of how it is put together, how the arguments are developed and what impact, overall, it is likely to have on the reader.

Finally, there is the revision stage and final editing. Here, the author takes special care over grammar, accuracy, style, vocabulary, sentence length, and so forth. Apart from the key questions mentioned above, these matters are dealt with in textbooks on writing.

In helping people to improve their writing skills, it is important to recognize that comments, criticisms and discussion at the planning, scanning and revision stages can be beneficial. But once the article or report is finalized, such comments are unwelcome. That is why it is important to get people to discuss documents at the earlier stages.

VOCABULARY AND SENTENCES

One of the most important ways to improve writing skills is to read a lot. Read material which contains the vocabulary you wish to absorb and use. If you want to write advertising material, select material you consider effective and read it through carefully. Notice the words used, the sentence lengths, the way arguments are developed, benefits presented, and so forth. Similarly, if you need to write articles for magazines, read the magazines in question. Notice the style, the words used, the way themes are developed in articles, over a number of issues. Study the advertisements in the magazines and see if you can build up pictures of typical readers.

Your selection of reading matter for news coverage and relaxation can help to improve vocabulary. Those who want to write for the general public might profitably read a popular newspaper regularly – recognizing that the words used and the way articles and news items are constructed are appropriate to the readership. If you want to appeal to a more up-market readership, read a serious newspaper. The same argument applies to magazines, novels, and the like. If you want to be a good writer, be a good reader!

When it comes to the writing process, some authors find it helpful to imagine that they are speaking to the person concerned, and then they write down what they say. This generally leads to a direct and clear form of writing, and a flowing style, but the draft produced will need careful and sensitive editing. The words and phrases we use in conversation are often made clearer by tone of voice and facial expression, which do not appear on the written page. The trick is to tighten up the grammar, but to leave intact the informality and immediacy of the spoken word.

One of the problems faced by new writers is that, when they read through material they have just written, they fail to notice errors or unclear statements. This is because we all have a tendency to see and hear what we expect, rather than what is there on the page. In essence we see what we wanted to say, rather than what we have written down. A way to reduce this effect, if you have the time, is to put a fair draft of the document in question on one side for a week or two. When this is brought out and read later, you are more likely to read it afresh, rather than remembering what you intended to say. Then it is easier to notice inconsistencies, duplications, errors, omissions and obscure passages.

PARTICULAR FORMATS

If you are writing an article for a magazine, you will need to follow the format as well as the style normally used in the particular publication. Reports, minutes of meeting and press releases all have their own structures. A detailed discussion of these is outside the scope of this book, but a few notes are provided on reports and press releases in Figure 27.

Figure 27

Notes on press releases
See that the press release is cleanly and accurately typed on good quality paper, double-spaced and with wide margins.

Write the press release as if you are a journalist writing for the newspaper or magazine where you would wish to see the item appear.

Open with the most newsworthy piece of information – one that captures the interest and imagination of the intended reader.

Make sure the essential facts are included: places, dates, times, and so forth. Often it is best to put these straight after the opening sentence, if they are not there.

Keep the headline simple and in keeping with the newspaper or journal you have in mind.

Keep punctuation simple and use capital letters only where this is really necessary.

Use single quotation marks for technical terms and double quotation marks for quoted speech.

Numbers one to nine should be typed in words; larger numbers in figures up to a million.

Try to keep the press release on one side of the paper only. If you want to give more details, put some notes on a second page so that the journalist can fill out the item if he or she wishes.

Notes on reports

Reports vary a good deal, but the following notes should prove a helpful framework for considering what sections you need and in what order.

If the report is long, give a one-page summary at the outset.

Open with a section setting out briefly the background to the report. Who asked for it? What is it intended to achieve?

Continue with a section on what you did to bring the report into existence: who was interviewed, what literature was consulted, what experiments were undertaken? If this is highly technical, summarize it in the text and put the detail in an appendix.

Follow this up with a section describing the results obtained. Don't muddy the waters with your interpretation of the data, just present it.

This should be followed by a section where you discuss the results, and explain your conclusions and any arguments you put forward to support them.

It is often helpful to bring together the key conclusions in a series of statements or in summary form.

There should be a section indicating what, in your view,

should follow. Are you recommending simply that people note the contents, or that action should be taken? If you recommend action, who should take it, and when?

A long report should have a table of contents between the title page and the summary – or even after the summary. Make sure the report is dated, and the authorship is clear. List references at the end.

ACTION GUIDELINES

1. Identify the key documents produced by your firm and who produces them.
2. Get out some of these documents and see if you are satisfied with them.
3. Where you see a need for improvement, help people through coaching and discussion to focus on the key issues: the intended readership, the message, the structure and the vocabulary.
4. Encourage appropriate reading.
5. Encourage a supportive climate where people are prepared to criticize each other's written work constructively, and where this criticism is accepted and considered seriously.
6. Consult specialist books on publicity material, report writing, writing minutes, etc.
7. Monitor improvements in the written work produced.

CHAPTER 18

DEVELOPING PEOPLE SKILLS

Interactions between people play a pretty big part in business. Take yourself, for example. In the course of your work, how many people do you have to deal with – in writing, by telephone or face to face? Take five minutes to jot down, as far as you can, the people you dealt with over the last four weeks (a look through your diary might give you a good start). Do you keep a list of the letters you receive and write? Add all these names to the list. Have you included the people in your firm? Does the list include customers, suppliers, advisers (accountant, bank manager)?

Select, say, seven of these people, those who are most important to your business. Now alongside each name, write down what you want from that person, in a word or phrase. You might write down 'orders for goods', 'fast delivery', 'high quality workmanship', 'sound advice'. If you are keen, try adding a third column: what do you think each person wants from you? In a phrase, you might write things like 'good quality products on time', 'prompt payments', 'good pay and recognition of good workmanship', 'attention to advice proffered'. Did you find it difficult to answer any of these questions? If so, you may find that your dealings with that person are not all they could be.

Similar lists could be written for everybody in your firm, although some of them would be a good deal shorter than yours. Some of the contacts between people are not all that crucial, but in any case effective communication and co-operation are essential to the success of your enterprise. Spending some time making sure that every employee, and especially each of your key people, has the ability to communicate can be an invaluable investment. Failures in communication can occur even when instructions are given clearly and people appear to be listening. That is because there is more to effective communication and collaboration than mere words.

SHARED OR COMPETING AIMS

In effect, every work-based relationship between two people is founded on two things: shared aims and/or competing aims. If the aims are shared, attention in the relationship needs to be focused on making sure that both parties agree about exactly what the aims are, and deciding together how these aims will be achieved. If there are competing aims, there must be negotiation and a recognition of the outcome each person expects of each activity. Let's clothe these general ideas with some examples.

If you visit a client who wants to buy some of your goods, your shared aim is to effect an agreement. However, there are potentially competing aims; for example, he or she would like a low price, and you would like a high one; he or she might prefer an early delivery date, but you would like more time to complete the order. There is nothing very mystical about all this, but if you want to be effective in dealing with people, recognizing these shared and competing aims is important.

Consider a more subtle example. Your foreman gets the maintenance people to set up a machine to make a certain component, and wants to leave the machine in this format all week. The machine takes two hours to set up. You know, however, that in order to satisfy your customers the machine should be making component A for two days a week, and component B for three days. Your aims are clear: satisfy the customer and make good use of the machine. Why does the foreman want to keep the machine on one setting all week? Will the change-over mean that he or she will have an unoccupied operative who might lose a bonus? Does the foreman have to go cap in hand to the maintenance people every time the machine is reset, an activity that he or she finds aggravating? Is he or she unaware of your schedule of delivery commitments to customers?

If you want full-hearted co-operation from this person, you need to think about his or her aims, and have a chat about the problems. Some of the issues which concern the foreman may not come to light in response to straight questions. To discover these you may need to listen very carefully, not only to what is said, but to the way it is said. Furthermore, you may need to listen carefully to recognize what is not being said. This ability to listen is absolutely central to improving your effectiveness in dealing with people.

There is a discussion of shared aims in connection with teamwork in Chapter 12.

LISTENING

In business, it is important to speak and write in ways that people understand, whether you are dealing with shareholders, customers, suppliers, employees or public officials. Part of the art of being understood is to recognize the way other people view the situation, their concerns and, in particular, what they expect of it. In this sense you can't really communicate effectively with anybody unless you listen first. Thus, in general, being effective in dealing with people means:

- listening to find out their views, concerns and aims
- recognizing where aims are shared and/or in conflict
- responding in an appropriate manner.

The question is, how can you learn this, and how can you ensure that your workforce learns how to deal with people? You will remember that to learn anything you have to respond to experience, and to develop skills you need to practise and to review the outcome of your activity. Learning how to interact with people follows this pattern. The key is twofold: (a) to be aware of what you are saying and doing; and (b) to have some way of recognizing how people are reacting, so that you can adjust your activities accordingly. This is a special kind of listening where we try to understand what people are thinking and feeling by observing not just what they say, but how they say it (eg, the expression on their face, and the way their hands and body move).

This is something we do automatically a lot of the time, but often we do it badly. Have you heard someone say, 'I thought that so-and-so was insensitive in the way he spoke to that fellow who just lost his wife'? What we mean is that the person listened to the words, but not the feelings of grief or loss that were evident to others. This is rather a dramatic example, but in everyday work we need to be sensitive to people's feelings and values if we are to communicate effectively with them.

Less dramatically, but equally devastating, is the way some managers deal with subordinates who make a mistake. Instead of thinking about, and being determined to avoid such mistakes in future, the rebuked individual comes away from the encounter feeling angry with the boss, and inclined more to revenge than reform. Such managers often fail to listen properly to exactly what happened and look for someone to blame, rather than trying to understand what went wrong, and all the circumstances, so as to avoid a recurrence. This problem also arises quite often when accidents are investigated.

ONE TO ONE

In every work-based activity involving more than one person, two things are going on side by side. The people concerned are performing a task of some kind, but at the same time there is a process of human interaction taking place. Improving the way people work together to achieve results means getting a handle on this interaction, so that the process can be 'matched' to the task.

One-to-one interactions vary from the casual greeting or short chat through to formal interviews. There are interviews for making sales (between the sales assistant and customer, or between the sales representative and purchasing officer, etc). If you and your people learn how to prepare for, and to conduct, purposeful conversations of various kinds, then your ability to deal with people in general should also improve.

Let's consider such a conversation or interview in stages as follows:

1. Preparing for the discussion.
2. Starting the discussion.
3. Covering the ground.
4. Ending the discussion.
5. Recording the results of the discussion.
6. Follow-up.

Short courses can be designed to cover these main points, and notes on these are given in Figure 28 (on page 160). The emphasis in such a course should be on learning how to become aware of the process of interaction, and to tailor one's own behaviour accordingly. Properly and sensitively used, a video recording of participants in such a course can be played back to help individuals see themselves in action and see where they can improve the way they come across to others. People don't suddenly become more effective after such courses; but by becoming aware of the processes involved, they should acquire the ability to use their everyday interactions with other people as a vehicle for learning how to improve. Their real improvement comes about on the job, over a period of time.

Figure 28 Interviews: key points

Preparation
Purpose of the interview?
Clarity of objectives/desired outcomes?
Identification of relevant topics to be covered?
Decision on appropriate structure?
Choice of suitable location?

Starting
Creation of atmosphere for constructive dialogue.
Ensuring interviewee aware of purpose of interview.
Reasonably prompt movement towards the business in hand.

Content
Asking appropriate questions.
Allowing/encouraging interviewee to do most of the talking.
Paying close attention to interviewee's perspective.
Ensuring any conclusions are soundly based.
Taking time to probe areas of weakness or lack of clarity.
Ensuring all points can be recalled later by interviewer.
Ensuring bias eliminated from any evaluations made.
Ensuring point-by-point build-up of data and evaluation.
Concentration on results, facts and behaviour.

Ending
Ensuring agreement on key facts, especially any to be recorded.
Ensuring agreement on any actions to be taken by either party.

Recording
Prompt, accurate recording of key facts established, agreements reached and actions to be taken.

Follow-up
Prompt implementation of agreed actions, and markers in the forward diary.

If several people attend such a course – perhaps your entire top team to start with – this is far more effective than sending one individual. A group of people in a small firm or department who understand something about the process can help each other to improve, whereas one person struggling alone can become discouraged.

The more practice you have at preparing for the work-based discussions and interviews you can foresee, the better equipped you will be for the ones that take you by surprise.

Suppose you can't afford the time or money to have a course. All is not lost, but the process of improving the interpersonal skills of the workforce will take longer. See if you can persuade a few of your colleagues to join you in working through the issues elaborated in Figure 28. In particular, one person in the group should practise observing the others' behaviour as you discuss the topics. Take turns at acting as observer, using one of the frameworks outlined below. This is a good way to start learning the listening skills we were talking about earlier.

OBSERVING GROUP BEHAVIOUR

The methods described here are rough guides only, but they are good enough to get a grip on what is happening in a given situation.

METHOD 1

Simply record each time a particular person speaks. Draw up a chart, and when a person speaks put a mark in the appropriate box.

METHOD 2

This is a little more difficult. Record the kind of statements made, but don't try to get down who spoke. Use the following five categories (although they will not fit well in every case): agreeing, disagreeing, building, questioning, proposing.

Agreeing and disagreeing are reasonably straightforward. Building means that what is said adds to an idea currently under discussion. Questioning means asking for clarification. If the question is really an attack on what has gone before, it is disagreeing. If a question is really suggesting something new (eg, 'Should we not be doing something different?'), this is classified as proposing. Proposing means suggesting that the discussion should start off in a new direction which does not add to current ideas being considered.

METHOD 3

You may improve on method 1 by trying to gain some estimate of the time each person speaks (eg, by putting more strokes for longer interventions). In method 1, a one-word interjection would count the same as a long speech.

METHOD 4

You may combine methods 1 and 2 by making a note against each person for the kind of intervention made each time.

METHOD 5

You may observe to whom each intervention is made. Is the speaker talking to the whole group, or to one member? Or does his or her attention seem to indicate that the person is talking to no one at all? Often a member of the group will address an individual when he or she is disagreeing violently with that person, or if he or she is seeking that person's support for his or her point of view. If someone seems to be talking to the air, maybe this is an indication that he or she has lost patience with the way the discussion is going.

A simple way of performing this type of analysis is to draw a sketch of the group, representing each member by a small circle. Then join each circle to the others by lines. Draw one short line pointing inwards to represent talking to the group as a whole, and one outwards to represent talking 'out of the group'. Record each intervention as a short stroke across the appropriate line – for example, for a word from A to B, put a short stroke across the line connecting A to B, etc.

METHOD 6

You may want to observe people's non-verbal behaviour. Do they seem interested, warmly supportive, violently opposed, utterly bored or totally uninterested? It is difficult to infer accurately what people feel, but you can often get some sense of whether people are giving their best or not.

Methods 3 to 6 are difficult to carry out properly, but each one gives you a little more insight into what is going on when a group of people get into a discussion.

REVIEWING INTERVIEWS

If you are able to observe one person interviewing another, you may learn something about the technique by observing what goes on, and in a training situation such observations can be fed back to the interviewer and interviewee to help them improve their performance in an interview.

To make the most of this opportunity, it is useful to have a structure for recording your observations. Note what kinds of remark are made, and how each person appears to react to these.

The framework given here can be used by someone observing a one-to-one interview, or (with some minor modification) by two people watching a video tape of themselves involved in a one-to-one interview. Observe the kinds of statement/question of the interviewer and the response of the interviewee at each stage of the discussion.

During the interview the discussion may be divided into stages such as: beginning; opening up; closing down; close. Alternatively there may be natural turning points in the discussion (eg, when the subject changes or when the interviewer moves systematically through a series of items to be considered).

Observe the non-verbal behaviour of the interviewer and interviewee. Consider to what extent you can infer the attitudes from these words and behaviours.

Write down what appears to you to have been the purpose of the discussion on the part of the interviewer and the interviewee respectively. If possible, when you have finished writing down your interpretation of their purposes, ask the interviewee what he or she saw as the aims of the discussion. Look back over your notes and consider to what extent the kinds of statement/question and response were conducive to the achievements of these purposes. As an extra check, look through the list of key points mentioned in Figure 28.

SUMMARY

1. Possible kinds of statement/question by the interviewer include:

- reflective – open
- probing – open
- probing – closed
- 'fixit' – solutions
- directive – assertive
- interpretative – judgmental

2. Possible kinds of response by interviewee include:

- agreeing – accepting
- disagreeing – disjointed
- building – expanding
- questioning – seeking clarification
- proposing – taking initiative

3. Possible kinds of behaviour of interviewer include:

- laid-back
- nodding assent
- leaning forward
- whole body movement
- benign smile
- interrupting
- frequent eye contact
- gazing into space

4. Possible kinds of behaviour of interviewee include:

- laid-back
- whole body movement

- head hung down
- speaking freely
- speaking hesitantly
- frequent eye contact
- averted eyes

5. Possible attitudes of interviewer include:

- relaxed
- supportive
- interested
- aggressive
- patronizing
- uninterested

6. Possible attitudes of interviewee include:

- relaxed
- open
- expansive
- defensive
- subservient
- aggressive

7. Possible purposes of interview discussion include:

- helping interviewee to learn and improve by reflecting on experience; considering personal style; analyzing work situation; reviewing how to deal with a work problem; drawing up an action plan
- helping interviewer explore the possibility of employing the interviewee; a subject using the knowledge of the interviewee; a problem using the expertise of the interviewee.

If you don't want to involve some of your colleagues in the learning exercise to begin with, you could try it alone, but that is a hard route and you will, most likely, not get far. Most people need the stimulus and encouragement of others.

Furthermore, it is the whole team that needs to be effective, not just one member. If you persist in going it alone, you need to 'step outside yourself' and observe how people are behaving in a given situation, to become aware of the process. For example, during a technical discussion you might stop trying to follow the arguments for a few minutes and ask yourself how each person is behaving: are his or her comments constructive, passively assenting or agreeing with some unspoken reservations which might give problems later on? The more you get switched on to how people react to ideas and to each other, the more effective you will become at managing them.

PEOPLE IN GROUPS

Often there is a need for two or three people to meet together for a discussion of some kind, or to be given some information that they all need. In larger organizations a lot of time is spent in such meetings because of the need to co-ordinate the activities of various people. Unfortunately, much of this time is wasted or fails to give full value because not enough thought has been given to the purpose of the meeting and how it should be conducted.

In any company, time wasted in meetings is costly, as the work of every person counts. Meetings need to be held from time to time, however, and it follows that there is value in learning together how to run an effective meeting, and how to behave to help achieve objectives. One way to learn about this is to run through the following checklist at the beginning of each meeting. This should not take long and will be worthwhile if you consider that there is a need to improve the effectiveness of meetings.

CHECKLIST FOR MEETINGS

1. At the beginning

- Is everyone clear about what the group is trying to achieve at the meeting?
- Is the procedure for running the meeting appropriate? NB: as an example, strong chairing and a rigid agenda may be good for a normal 'business' meeting, but not much good if you need creative, imaginative solutions to problems.

2. At the end

- Is everybody clear about what will happen next?
- Does everybody know what they have to do now?
- Was the time spent on the meeting used well?
- Are there ways in which the conduct of such a meeting might be improved next time?

3. When bogged down

- The discussion seems to be going over the same ground again. Is somebody unhappy with a decision made a few minutes ago?
- Are there disagreements about the basic facts?
- Does somebody feel that their point of view has not been properly considered?
- Can the group reach agreement about what is to be achieved, what has been achieved/agreed and how to proceed?

When the group begins to get the idea, a member might interrupt the discussion with a question like, 'Do we feel that the way we are tackling this discussion is the most effective? As group members become more conscious of the desired outcomes of the meeting, and also more tuned into the process, the meetings themselves will become more businesslike and productive. Once again, this process can be started and given impetus by a short course.

INTERACTING GROUPS

In some organizations, people who work in sections can see themselves as separate groupings, with interests and concerns that differ from those of others. This can even occur in small firms where two different kinds of operation are conducted by two different groups of people (eg, where you have one group of people at the factory making products, and another group 'on the road' as travelling salespeople). This is not mainly a matter of personalities, although this can come into it, as people who like to go out and sell often have different personalities compared to people who like to work at machines or at a desk.

Apart from such factors, there are differences that arise purely from the jobs they do, and the pressures and concerns arising from these jobs.

Problems sometimes arise in terms of relationships between such groups of people, but this need not be the case. They each have a part to play in the firm's success, and the important thing is to help people to see the overall picture and how the contribution of each section and individual fits in.

If necessary, you can arrange meetings between such groups of people, provided you lead the meetings with care. Draw up an agenda and create an atmosphere where everybody is looking to the future rather than the past; for ways to solve problems and to work together effectively, rather than apportioning blame or repeating allegations of incompetence. As in any situation where success depends on collaboration, getting the people involved to identify their shared goals is a pre-requisite of success.

NEGOTIATING

To the extent that the people you are dealing with do not share your aims, you are effectively in a negotiating situation. We generally use the term 'negotiating' when employers and trade union leaders try to reach agreement about pay and working conditions, or where a salesperson is seeking a deal with a client. In reality, people spend a good deal of their time negotiating, because this occurs whenever what one person wants to achieve in a given situation does not coincide with what other people want out of it.

Suppose you go to an employee and ask him or her to work overtime for an hour, that evening. If the employee wants to work overtime (eg, if he or she has no appointments, would be paid and would welcome the money) your aims are shared. But if it is his or her wedding anniversary, some persuasion is called for on your part if he or she is to stay. You are, in effect, now in a negotiating position. What you offer in this situation may have nothing to do with work, or pay. What you offer should reflect the employee's needs and wants. Offering to run the employee home in the car to give him or her more time at home to prepare to go out might suffice.

If you want to gain people's co-operation, you need to look at the situation from their point of view. This is one of the key points to learn if you want to succeed in negotiation, of whatever sort. In practice, insofar as the result depends on you, effective negotiation depends on two things: how well you prepare, and how well you conduct yourself during the interview. If the other party does not want a settlement, persists in unreasonable demands or is unwilling to give to you the items you consider essential, then there cannot be a satisfactory deal.

The elements of negotiation – preparation and conduct – can be covered in short courses, but to become proficient you and your people will need to follow up both the way people prepare for negotiation, and also the way people conduct themselves. Coaching is a most valuable method to use here (see Chapter 15).

To reinforce the learning about preparatory work, get each of your people concerned into the habit of jotting down short notes prior to any negotiation, and talking through their preparatory work with a colleague. There are three good reasons for doing this. First, the person concerned will probably pick up some points which will enable him or her to improve the preparation. Second, the person concerned will learn how to prepare better: even when no extra ideas are brought out in discussion, the review of the original points will reinforce learning and fix them more firmly in the individual's mind. Third, the person who is consulted will learn something.

Be sensible about all this. If the negotiations concerned are routine, reviews of this kind can become repetitive and boring. This can be overcome to some extent by using a different person to talk it through, and by using only selected instances, rather than every one.

How can you reinforce learning about how to conduct negotiations? Once again we are concerned with interaction between people, and in particular with the ability to listen. One way to go about this is to have a colleague accompany the 'negotiator' during discussions with the other party. The colleague who goes along should concentrate on noticing the interactions, what your man or woman says, how the other person reacts to that, and how your negotiator handles that reaction. Afterwards, the two of them can talk over what happened and, using this, can both learn how to improve their handling of negotiating situations.

The learning procedure just described is asking a lot of your people. Before you can expect to try this and make it work, an atmosphere of trust must be developed. People must develop some skills in listening and observing behaviour, and in helping each other to learn.

ACTION GUIDELINES

1. Consider the key working relationships in your business. Ensure that those of your people who are involved – buyers, receptionists, salespeople, van drivers – learn how to use contacts.
2. Learn to listen and help your staff develop this skill to a high standard.
3. Learn to prepare for one-to-one discussions and interviews so that each event becomes more productive, and help your staff do the same.
4. Learn to manage groups of people in discussions and decision meetings, so that time together is purposeful and productive.
5. If you have distinct groups of people, recognize that some differences of view are inevitable. Use this as a strength rather than regarding it merely as a problem.
6. Learn to prepare thoroughly for negotiations and train your key people to do the same.

CHAPTER 19

CREATIVITY AND INNOVATION

How can you ensure that your company keeps one jump ahead of the competition? This depends on being sensitive to the market-place and the changing desires and requirements of the people who buy your products and services, and spotting gaps in the current range of goods and services available. There may be a need to develop the quality and range of your products and services in the light of these market trends, or to find ways of reducing prices, improving delivery time, streamlining packaging or increasing advertising. No doubt the majority of these changes can be brought about by analyzing the problems and developing straightforward solutions to them.

You may, however, want to run a firm where people are on the look-out for new ways of achieving results, and for new products and services which can be offered in the market-place. You may not be content with straightforward solutions, and feel that to give your firm the competitive edge, you want some creative ideas generated, and you want to see them brought into operation in practical terms.

Within organizations it is important to distinguish between creativity – the generation of new ideas and approaches – and innovation – getting new ideas off the ground in practical terms. Some people are good at coming up with ideas, but never seem to get around to putting them to good use. There are also people around who do not generate ideas, but when they are fired with enthusiasm, can make things happen.

How can you develop, with your own people, the ability to create and innovate? In one sense it is not possible to develop this ability, since if people are incapable of having many ideas there's no way forward. However, under the right conditions, many people are capable of generating new ideas and putting them into practice. The secret of success lies in taking action in two main areas: first, to stimulate people to think in this way; and second, to remove the many constraints which hamper such thinking and behaviour. In many ways it is necessary to consider removing the barriers before stimulating people to think and act creatively, because if you do it the other way round their enthusiasm can be dampened by the obstacles and difficulties they face.

BARRIERS TO CREATIVITY

A director once said to me, 'These managers who work for me never come up with any ideas at all'. Studying the director in action, it did not take long to understand why. Any ideas put forward were immediately criticized, and at no time was consideration given to plans or activities in the light of anything said by any of the managers. Plans were always announced to the managers by the director, who would allow questions for clarification, but not any questions or comments which might conceivably lead to changes. In such a situation there really was no point whatever in managers being creative: suggesting ideas was virtually a punishable offence.

The fact of the matter is that for most people creativity is generally like a tender plant: easily crushed by harsh criticism and withered by the fire of a hostile reaction. People who put forward ideas generally do not mind much if their ideas are ultimately rejected – but what they find intolerable is when what they have to suggest is not seriously *considered*. If not one of their ideas is ever picked up and used in some way, they will eventually get the message.

Thus, removing the barriers to creativity is all about the boss being prepared to:

- listen
- encourage other people to listen
- make some use of every viable and potentially useful idea
- make it clear that he or she has acted on someone's idea
- give credit and praise where they are due
- make it clear to people that good ideas can be made to work.

Over a period of time (these things do not happen overnight), the act of listening and encouraging others to listen will create a new atmosphere in the firm, and people who have ideas will be willing to put them forward. The more outrageous and, at first hearing, nonsensical ideas people are prepared to put forward, provided they are seriously meant, the more successful you will have been at developing a creative 'culture' – 'the way we do things around here'.

If you want to accelerate this process, have a meeting with your senior people, and start a discussion on the question, 'How can we encourage each other, and our workforce, to put forward new and imaginative ideas to improve the business?' Don't put forward any ideas yourself. Get your people to suggest them, and work out together how you will try to put a few of them into practice. You could use the brainstorming technique below.

Apart from the discouragement of having ideas squashed, you will have problems if it seems impossible to carry them through to fruition. The word 'seem' is important. When you are talking about how people behave, how things seem to them is often more important than how things really are. If something is actually possible, but it seems impossible to a person, it is this perception which will influence the person's behaviour. Thus, it must not merely be possible for people to bring about change – they must realize that it can be done.

STIMULATING CREATIVITY

Suppose you have made a good start at breaking down the barriers to creativity. How do you get people started on suggesting and refining new ideas? First of all, you must recognize that the generation of new ideas means somehow jerking them out of the rut of thinking as they always think. Without stimulation most people tend to draw on their experiences and on their repertoire of solutions and ideas they have used before. With training, people can learn to analyze problems and devise solutions, but devising novel ideas is a different ball game.

BRAINSTORMING

One of the most common methods of jerking people out of a rut is called 'brainstorming'. Training a number of people how to brainstorm can make a big difference to the way your firm operates because, besides being a useful technique, it encourages people to be more open to new ideas from whatever source. Some people seem to think that brainstorming is just a structureless free-for-all. It is not. It is a carefully thought out process for developing new approaches and ideas; and if it is going to work, the process must be taken one step at a time.

The first step is to gather together a suitable small group of people to work on the matter you wish to tackle in an imaginative way. Make sure that everyone who is taking part really understands the challenge or problem to be tackled. Start with a discussion about this, if necessary, and let people ask 'idiot questions'. Allow any questions, however irrelevant they may seem. Such questions matter to the people who pose them. Make sure that every issue and concern is surfaced. If you find that you need more information (eg, about the potential customers for the new product you hope to design, or about the availability and cost of raw materials) make arrangements to get it.

Having prepared the ground in this way, the next step is to get the group to suggest ideas. Get the group members to express these in single words or short phrases, and immediately write these down on flip charts. No explanations of the ideas, comments, questions or criticisms are allowed at this stage. Encourage a quick uninterrupted flow of suggestions, however crazy or odd they might seem. Get all these down in writing where everybody can see them. When the flow of ideas begins to slow down, move to the next step.

Request explanations of each item on the list. Invite the person who suggested each item to briefly explain what he or she meant. Again, no comments or criticisms are allowed, but group members can ask questions for clarification, to make sure that they understand what is being proposed, and what idea is being expressed. By going through the list of items one by one, hopefully a number of people will be able to join in the discussion as it proceeds. Sometimes new ideas come up at this stage. List them for discussion.

When every idea listed has been explained, go back down the list and discuss items in depth. Now criticism and comment are appropriate, and ideas which prove really impractical can be discarded. Criticism too early in the process brings with it the danger that good ideas will be discarded because members of the group did not really understand what is being proposed, and did not take the trouble to think carefully about it. The more original and novel ideas are the most likely to be lost through early and uninformed criticism. Premature criticism ensures that only mediocre ideas survive.

The final step is to select ideas for practical development – for example, research into new products and services, progressively narrowing down the field as your requirements on attractiveness, cost and quality are taken fully into account.

OTHER APPROACHES

There are other ways of stimulating creativity (eg, 'synectics' or 'lateral thinking'). If you really want new ideas, it is worth investigating these techniques and arranging training in their use for key members of your staff. In each case the basic idea is to help people to look at situations and problems in totally new ways, so that they can find solutions and ways of achieving results that do not follow the normal 'logic' of step-by-step problem-solving (eg, gathering data, analysis, postulating alternatives, evaluating possible outcomes and selecting the optimum course of action).

It is impossible to do justice to these techniques in a few words, but in synectics the group members are helped to understand the psychological processes involved in creative thinking so that they can become more effective individually and in the group. In practice, when tackling a particular subject, the problem is first reviewed and reduced to its essentials in discussion, and then an analogy is sought between the key elements of the problem. This analogy is explored in special ways. It is this 'excursion' which enables people to view situations and problems from a new perspective. Finally, participants in the process reconsider the original problem in the light of the insights received during the excursion – sometimes with very helpful and unexpected results.

The synectics approach seeks to release people from the constraints of 'rational' thinking which limit them to known, safe statements. It enables them to break out of their stereotypes and to widen the areas for further action. A word of warning: you need a good tutor to train people in synectics.

Some people do not regard lateral thinking as the same as creativity, but in practical terms it enables people to formulate solutions to problems which do not follow normal logic. In effect, it enables people to see problems from new angles, and in this sense it certainly is creative. In essence, lateral thinking is concerned with using various tools which enable individuals to go against the rules of logical thinking. These tools have the effect of:

- highlighting the dominant features of a problem and rejecting ideas which inhibit new thinking
- viewing the problem from a number of novel viewpoints
- loosening up the constraints on free thinking
- deliberate use of chance.

Whatever approaches you decide to use, remember to reduce the barriers to creativity first. Involve a number of people in any training or development work you do, to enhance creativity so that the people involved will be able to help and encourage each other.

BARRIERS TO INNOVATION

Like creativity, innovation is an untidy business. What stops people from doing things in your organization? Probably one of the major constraints is the very tidiness that arises when the firm becomes too paperbound and systematic in the way it conducts its business and internal affairs. Once systems become established, people prefer not to change them. Most people like the procedures they know about and are happy to use. They dislike change and disruption in their work patterns and take refuge in the routine.

The evidence is clear. If you want a routine task done competently, consistently and repeatedly, go for a simple, clear system and train people to use it properly. But do not expect, under these conditions, that new ideas will emerge and be put into effect. The likelihood is that they will not. Do you manage in a nice cosy way where everybody agrees with every change in machinery, layout or procedure before it is introduced? This may be a recipe for harmony, but not for innovation and progress.

Are you very cost-conscious and penny-pinching, applying cost control methods in fine detail? You may be in control, but if you carry this philosophy too far you will fail, because your success depends on keeping close to the customer and keeping ahead – you can't achieve that by saving every penny. Innovation is disruptive, disturbing, potentially upsetting, as cherished procedures that seem to work, and that were devised with great care, now come under threat. Can you handle that? The idea is not to cause disruption, but to manage that which arises in the wake of innovation; not to generate unease, but to accept change and to enable people to cope with it (see Chapter 10).

The barriers to innovation are in people, their attitudes and their attachment to known methods and machinery, and to comfortable procedures where they know just what to expect. You may say that innovation often costs money and that the lack of cash is the barrier. But the fact of the matter is that, by and large, dedicated people, uninhibited by their attachment to the past or to current practice, will overcome problems of finance. People who have got a good idea and really want to see it through will generally find a way.

You need to create a culture where those who innovate are thought of as the 'good guys', and regarded as contributing something of real value to the firm. You must back them. People who innovate will fail sometimes. Can you take that? Many major innovations have succeeded only after a series of failures. If the failure of a serious attempt at innovation is 'punished', and regarded as unhelpful, this forms an effective barrier to further innovative efforts. Failures should be accepted as part of the price of being in a challenging business – provided the level of investment (the risk) was containable and worth taking in the light of the potential rewards.

In summary, removing the barriers to innovation involves:

- enabling people to accept that methods and machinery must change if the firm is to survive and prosper
- helping people realize that positive innovation will enhance the future prospects of the firm and their own jobs
- encouraging people to loosen up procedures and to be prepared to take calculated business risks in trying out new ideas (*not* risks in the health and safety area)
- enabling people who innovate to cope with failure, to analyze what went wrong and to start again if they have a promising idea

- encouraging people to accord respect and esteem to those who seek to innovate
- providing personal support and backing to the innovators.

STIMULATING INNOVATION

Given that you are generating ideas, and have removed the barriers, how do you promote innovation? The one thing that does not seem to work well is to press-gang people into spearheading innovation. What you need is volunteers who are likely to be winners. And they need backers.

What are the qualities to look for in 'winning volunteer innovators'? There does not seem to be a simple answer. There are, however, some clues to what to look for in such a person. Does he or she really believe in the idea underlying the innovation? Does he or she behave in a manner that convinces you that he or she really wants the idea to work out in practice. (Remember that some 'ideas people' are content to toy with their thoughts: deep down they don't really care whether the idea is put to practical use or not. Don't back people like that. Able they might be; dedicated they are not.)

The innovator is often not the person who originated the idea, but rather somebody who is fired with its practicality and utility. That is what you are looking for, a person with his or her head in the clouds, but with both feet firmly planted on solid ground; somebody who delights in seeing things happen. In larger organizations, people like that need a senior person as a backer, to help them deal with the system; to help them obtain resources and gain co-operation from people. In the small firm, it will generally be the boss who has to help smooth the pathway a little, provided he or she has the right attitude, as outlined above.

In larger organizations, it may be necessary to find senior managers who are sympathetic to innovation and then to have one or two innovators loosely reporting to them. Such senior managers will have the muscle to 'make room' for the innovators, to enable them to gain access to information, resources and the help they need to push changes through the system. Particularly in large organizations, innovators need this kind of backing to succeed.

CLIMATE

In seeking to promote learning for creativity and innovation, as in so many areas, the attitude of the boss is crucial. He or she must have the ability to create an atmosphere where purposeful novelty is regarded as the normal way to make progress.

ACTION GUIDELINES

1. Decide whether you want to stagnate or to create and innovate.
2. If you want a creative, innovative firm, start to dismantle the barriers to new thinking and action.
3. Encourage people at all levels to put forward ideas for consideration – and don't brush them aside.
4. Take positive steps to open up people's minds to new ways of looking at the firm's products, services and procedures.
5. Back people who have a sound idea which they want to see brought to fruition in a practical way.
6. Encourage people who fail in the attempt, recognizing that success is often born of the experiences gained in failure; use this as a learning opportunity.

CHAPTER 20

KEEPING AHEAD OF THE FIELD

By now, you have probably concluded that there are several things you can do to improve the effectiveness of your firm, or your particular department at the very least. You will probably find that many improvements are desirable; but a key question is, which of these are essential, and likely to enhance the effectiveness of the firm? You will need to take a short-term view, then a long-term view, of all this. Are there areas which crucially affect your survival in the short run? These must be tackled first. If your market is haywire, your quality just not good enough or your money-management lacking, you must develop the competence of the key people concerned – double quick. There's no point in creating grandiose training schemes for the future of the firm if it is in danger of imminent collapse.

Don't leave it there, however. Once you have a reasonable prospect of survival, devote some of your attention to the longer-term investment in people. If you can't spare the time to invest in people, then you had better make a start, in earnest, in dealing with your own competence in managing and using your time (see Chapter 11).

People development should be managed, just as every other activity in a well-run firm is managed. The way it is managed should be consistent with the methods used in other parts of the business. In the case of small and medium-sized firms, this means the minimum of paperwork and the maximum of communication and trust between people. Nevertheless, informality should not equate to sloppiness. There should be a clear understanding of the purposes of development, decisions about priorities and agreed action and expectations.

In larger firms there needs to be some system. You must be

seen to be fair and you will need a way to record what is happening, otherwise the movement of people may obscure problems of people development. But even here, make sure that it is the management, starting at the very top, which is managing people development and using the systems, and not the other way round.

The key decisions are, therefore, connected with the areas of improvement which are really important for you; where to start; and how to ensure that worthwhile learning is taking place and making a real difference to the way the firm operates.

PRIORITIES

What are the most urgent areas where you and your people need to perform more effectively? There are two ways into this problem. The first method focuses on the current problems of the firm, whereas the second approach is to take a thorough look at each aspect of operation. Use the problem-centred approach first so that urgent matters are covered.

Once you have identified some priorities from this approach you can work on these, while at the same time starting to examine operations of the firm step by step in a systematic way. Many of the needs you identify from the systematic method are likely to be similar to those arising from the problem-centred approach, and you might well be tempted to miss out the second step. *Don't.* Often, key issues are unearthed by the systematic method. Furthermore, you will learn a good deal about the way your firm operates by working through things systematically. As a by-product, you will probably find better ways of doing things as well.

If you already know a good deal about the intimate workings of the firm, the systematic approach will not take long, and will act as a useful check and complement to the problem-centred approach.

Choosing priorities for action is not something you should do alone, unless your firm is very small indeed. Involve other people, both to gain their commitment, and to improve the quality of your choices. The way you involve people depends on your circumstances, but at the very least you should tell them what you are about and seek their views about ways of improving the firm, including areas where further learning will help bring these improvements about.

You may also find it helpful to talk over some of your firm's or your department's problems with friends or fellow business-people whom you trust – perhaps members of your local chamber of commerce or business club, or members of the local branch of a professional or trade body to which you belong.

PROBLEM-CENTRED APPROACH

This approach is summarized in Figure 29. The word 'problem' here means anything that stops the firm from performing well. It could be concerned with the market-place, processing of information, raw materials, lack of space or a host of other constraints. At first sight some of these may seem inappropriate, in that they seem to be outside the control of your department or your firm. But success in business is all about coping with reality and seeing what you and your people can do to overcome such problems. Many managers have found that when they examine problems in depth there are ways to improve and to influence decisions which beforehand seemed intractable.

Having got your list, take the problem you consider most pressing, and look at question 1 in Figure 29: 'How do people see the problem?' Often, problems are spelt out in vague terms. Talk them over with some of your colleagues in the firm, including those most concerned, and see how far you can pin this down to specifics. Don't be content with statements like, 'We need to get orders processed more quickly'. A specific statement is, 'Our customers complain if they have to wait more than a week or so for us to respond to their orders'.

The advantage of being specific is that it compels you to consider alternatives and what, realistically, can be done about the problem. Is it fair for customers to expect this standard? Have you or your people made rash promises? Could you re-educate your customers to expect slower deliveries – perhaps with some compensating factor like lower price or higher quality? Or must you examine your work practices?

Question 2 ('What would be a satisfactory state of affairs?') is another way to sharpen things up. State what you consider to be a viable situation. To consider the above illustration, you might well say here, 'We must ensure that we respond to every order within seven days'. The great thing here is to have a verifiable, achievable target for performance. It is essential to discuss this with the people concerned to ensure that they consider the target reasonable. Nothing is so disheartening as

Figure 29 Learning needs: problem-centred approach

List each of the main problems faced by your firm at the present time. For each problem answer the following questions:

1. Discuss the problem as you see it with other people in the firm. How do people see the problem?
2. If the problem could be solved, what would be the new situation? What would be a satisfactory state of affairs? Describe it.
3. What is considered to be behind the problem?
4. What section/s of the firm are involved?
5. Which particular people are involved?
6. What competences will people need if this problem is to be solved?
7. How can people acquire the knowledge, skills and insights necessary to solve the problem?

The answers to these questions will help you to draw up a plan.

being pressed constantly to do the impossible. Alternatively, it soon gets boring if you set the targets too low in relation to the resources available.

At this stage you may be wondering what this has got to do with learning, training and development. The point is that if you need to improve performance or change procedure, people need to learn how to do what is required. Some of this learning will be quick and easy, but some people may require help from you if they are to learn quickly.

Questions 3 and 4 are concerned with locating the underlying cause of the problem and are intended to make you think more deeply about just who is involved in operational terms. The trouble is that we often fail to look beyond the obvious. Take the above illustration a step further. Is the problem of slow deliveries a matter of how the information is handled (who opens the letters and passes orders on to despatch), or a shortage of finished goods in stock? If you speed up to a seven-day turn-around, will you need to keep higher stocks of raw materials?

It must come down to some people in particular who have to

increase throughput, reduce wastage or improve decision-making (question 5). Be very careful indeed to ensure that this is presented to people as an exciting upgrading of the situation, not as action taken to remedy some defect on their part. (Unfortunately, people sometimes resent training as indicating that somehow they are not up to scratch. This attitude undermines the effectiveness of training programmes. Encourage a positive attitude to learning and training.)

Then there is a need to specify competences (question 6). 'Joe Bloggs should be able to cope with packaging up to 16 typical orders a day': this means he must be able to identify each item requested and locate it in the stores without delay. He must be able to select appropriate packaging materials (padded bags or cartons, say), assemble the items in a reasonable shape for posting, insert padding as required, seal, weigh and add the required postage. In more complex cases you may need to break the tasks down into smaller steps (see Chapter 16).

Be as specific as you can. In some jobs, performance can't be sensibly specified in numbers. It is not just how quickly a telephone operator deals with an enquiry or puts it through to the appropriate person in the firm – clarity of speech and politeness matter just as much, but can't usefully be expressed in numbers. Even with salespeople, where numerical statements of amounts sold are possible, it would be short-sighted to focus on this factor alone. In some cases you will need to help teams of people develop skills together.

Finally (question 7), you must decide on what methods will be used to help bring about this learning in each case. Remember that learning takes place when people respond to what they are reading, hearing or seeing. If skills are required, there needs to be a build-up from simple elements to the full task, practice followed by knowledge of results, and some indication of what to do next to improve performance.

Bear in mind that skills take longer to acquire than knowledge, but that knowledge is quickly forgotten by most people unless it is constantly used or revised. Use a sensible mixture of off-the-job education or training mingled with on-the-job instruction and coaching, bearing in mind that much of the specific knowledge needed by the workers in your organization comes from you and your senior colleagues.

There are now a number of 'open learning' resources and flexible learning arrangements available to enable you and your people to learn at home or at your workplace, at your own pace and at times convenient to you. Most adults will need the stimulus and encouragement of a tutor or other learners, and if there are several people using such methods it may be useful to set aside a room where they can work – individually – on their learning materials. Learners can often help each other, even if they are studying totally different subjects. It is the opportunity to talk over a point with someone, helping the learner to think things through, or to discuss a practical problem concerned with organizing study, which people find helpful.

According to the methods you choose, the study room might need to be equipped with an audio tape recorder, a videoplayer and monitor, a suitable computer, and so forth. There are now a number of useful computer programmes in subjects as diverse as management accounting, keyboard skills and foreign language vocabulary. With many of these flexible learning packages there is an opportunity to contact an experienced specialist tutor – either by telephone or by making an appointment, and this will generally be necessary if there is no expert in the subject available in your company.

DEVELOPMENT PLAN

The easiest way to draw up a plan is to follow the systematic approach outlined in Figure 30. If this deals only with formal training, it will amount to what is called a 'training plan'. But if you want to develop your people to the full, you will not take such a narrow view of things. Formal training is only one way of helping people learn. On its own it has limited value. The important thing is to get people learning and helping each other learn as part of the way the business is run.

Figure 30 Learning needs: systematic method

1. Draw up a simple diagram of the way people are organized in your firm.
2. Make a list of the key jobs that have to be done, and who does them.
3. For each key job, write down the main tasks and what you expect to be done.
4. Consider each area of the business and write down what improvements, if any, you would like to see over a period.

5. For each area where you would like to see an improvement, after discussions with the people concerned, answer the following questions:
   What improvement is needed?
   Who is involved?
   For each person involved, what do they need to learn?
   How will they learn this? (Specify any training planned using work experience, books or coaching.)
   Who will conduct the training/coaching?
   When will this learning take place, and by what date is it expected to bear fruit?
   How much will this cost, and what benefits do you expect?
6. It will become clear that you cannot do all that you would like at once, and in choosing your time scales for each item you will need to take this into account. Add a note on how you intend to train any new people you appoint. Put this together with the items from the preceding section and you have a plan to develop the firm by developing the key people in it.
7. Make sure that someone accepts responsibility for ensuring that these learning programmes are followed through – modifying them, if necessary, as the nature of the work changes. Keep a simple record of this activity.

Thus, what you need is not a training plan, but a development plan to put your firm ahead. Training may have an important part to play, but the name of the game is not training, but learning to develop the business and the competence of its people. (Question 1 in Figure 30 asks you to sketch out, in diagrammatic form, the key jobs in your firm. See Figure 31 as an illustration of the kind of diagram you need.)

In answer to question 2 in Figure 30, you will need to write down what you expect the person concerned to do. In a small company, you might write down for the company secretary, for example: 'Ensure that the financial and administrative affairs of the company are properly recorded and conducted in accordance with all legal requirements, and that the directors have the financial information needed to run the business effectively – including cost information, projected cashflow forecasts and full information on current and impending legislation and related requirements pertinent to the company's business'. In a medium-sized firm there might be a separate finance director to undertake some of these duties.

Figure 31 Key jobs

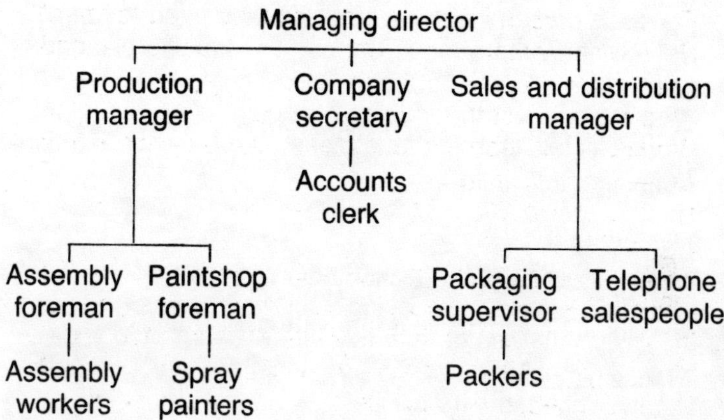

For the production manager you might write something like: 'Ensure that production is properly planned and carried out in a cost-effective manner, providing good quality products in time to meet demand'. Definitions of this kind do not cover everything, but they should be enough to stimulate a constructive discussion with the person concerned about what you expect, and what he or she needs to know to do the job properly. During such a discussion, a much clearer picture of the requirements of the job should emerge. Some people write this out and call it a job description, but unless you intend to replace the person concerned, this written document is scarcely worth the effort of writing it: it is the *discussion* which is important. In a smaller firm, the job will be changing constantly and a written job description could prove to be a nuisance.

What you need next is an agreed plan, based on these discussions, to bring about improvements in the way the firm is run in each of these areas. This means that the learning and the development of the firm will go hand in hand.

The next part is difficult if you have not done it before. Earlier in this book we discussed various areas of the business and provided checklists and ideas to get you started. The kind of area you will need to cover depends on the nature of your business, but your coverage is likely to include some of the following topics:

- Marketing and selling.
- Business planning.
- Managing money.
- Assuring quality.
- Managing transport and distribution.
- Managing information.
- Health and safety.
- Managing change and technology.
- Developing creativity and innovation.
- Managing people.

As you select each area for attention, reflect on what improvements you would like to see – in specific terms. Identify the people at the heart of the activity, and consider what improvements in their skills, knowledge and attitudes would bring benefit to the firm. Talk these matters over with the people concerned, asking them for their own ideas on how improvements can be brought about, and offer to help them to succeed by coaching and offering training.

Make sure you emphasize the positive, forward-looking approach to the problem. You are not looking for people who are doing things *wrong*, but for people who, with help, can do *better*. They should see the offer of training as a positive reward because they show potential, not as a punishment for their inadequacies. Your positive approach and attitude are vital: people will derive very limited benefit from training if they do not feel a desire to engage in it and expect to benefit from it (see Chapter 14).

In some cases you may want to encourage people to study for examinations so that they can be better qualified to undertake their jobs. When they attend classes, such people will probably meet with others doing similar jobs, and this could bring some new, useful ideas into the business. The education and training they receive should enable them to look more broadly and critically (in the positive sense) at the way your firm does things, and thus suggest ways to improve the products or services you offer, or the way you organize your information or production methods. Be open to consider such ideas.

If you are running the kind of organization that welcomes learning and new ideas, all this will help you to stay ahead of the field. You will need to give special attention to newcomers in your plan.

USING EXTERNAL RESOURCES

It is always a problem to know when to use the services of outsiders – colleges, training organizations, consultants, and so forth. Deciding which ones to use is an even bigger problem. There has been a vast increase in the number of organizations offering such help, and there are now lists and registers you can consult, often through your local library, trade association, professional body, chamber of commerce or business club.

You will need to use outside resources when the knowledge or expertise you need does not exist in the firm, or when the skill to be developed would be too expensive or slow to achieve by using your own resources. For example, you may not be able to train someone to operate a keyboard properly, but this could be done by a training body because they can organize a class made up of people from several firms. If you want someone to attain a qualification, they will generally need training with a university or college.

When it comes to making a choice, there really is no substitute for a recommendation from people you trust. There are two key questions to consider:

1. Does this course cover the ground my firm needs?
2. Do the people running the course (a) know the subject, and (b) have the ability to put it over to the people I want to attend the course?

These are the questions you should put to other people who have used the trainers concerned. You might consult your trade or professional body or local businesspeople, if you think they have the experience and expertise to help you make these judgments. When you or your people return from a course, you need to consider what they have learned and whether the course gave you value for money.

MONITORING PROGRESS

There is no need to make a meal of this. Simple records of the courses people have attended and how the cost worked out will be valuable information. The more important consideration is whether your people develop the ability to undertake their work more effectively, and how this feeds through into better products and services to your customers and lower operating costs – and thus a more profitable and healthy business.

In larger organizations, there is a tendency for operational pressures to squeeze out training so that people do not actually attend the courses as agreed. If this is a problem in your organization, then someone needs to keep a central record of who should attend courses, and make the necessary arrangements. If someone over-rules this decision and prevents an individual from attending the course (eg, by pleading some unforeseen operational factor), they should be made to account for this in writing, and then in person, to the chief executive or managing director. If the chief executive takes the firm seriously, he or she will take the development of the people seriously too, and will see to it that only in the most exceptional situations does training give way to operational needs. To do otherwise is tantamount to eating the seed corn – a short-term expedient leading to long-term disaster.

Remember the power of example, and the power of praise. If *you* want to learn to improve, and if *you* recognize the achievements of others, they will want to follow your lead.

ACTION GUIDELINES

1. Identify areas where you would like your firm or department to be more effective.
2. Talk this through with the people concerned.
3. Agree an improvement plan with them. Help and encourage people to acquire levels of skill and knowledge that will enable them to achieve their goals.
4. Help people use appropriate learning methods, making use of formal training, coaching and external resources according to need.
5. Monitor progress, setting an example and giving praise and encouragement where due.

Index